Microsoft

D1535876

MOS 2016 Study Guide for Microsoft Access

John Pierce

Microsoft Office Specialist
Exam 77-730

MOS 2016 Study Guide for Microsoft Access
Published with the authorization of Microsoft Corporation by:
Pearson Education, Inc.

ISBN-13: 978-0-7356-9939-7
ISBN-10: 0-7356-9939-9

Library of Congress Control Number: 2016953083

1 16

For information about buying this title in bulk quantities, or for special sales
opportunities (which may include electronic versions; custom cover designs;
and content particular to your business, training goals, marketing focus,
or branding interests), please contact our corporate sales department at
corpsales@pearsoned.com or (800) 382-3419.

For government sales inquiries, please contact governmentsales@pearsoned.com.

For questions about sales outside the U.S., please contact intlcs@pearson.com.

Editor-in-Chief
Greg Wiegand

Senior Acquisitions Editor
Laura Norman

Senior Production Editor
Tracey Croom

Editorial Production
Online Training Solutions, Inc.
(OTSI)

**Series Project Editor/
Proofreader**
Kathy Krause (OTSI)

Technical Editor
Joan Lambert (OTSI)

Compositor/Indexer
Susie Carr (OTSI)

Copy Editor
Jaime Odell (OTSI)

Editorial Assistant
Cindy J. Teeters

Interior Designer
Joan Lambert (OTSI)

Cover Designer
Twist Creative • Seattle

Contents

What do you think of this book? We want to hear from you!

Microsoft is interested in hearing your feedback so we can improve our books and learning resources for you.
To participate in a brief survey, please visit:

https://aka.ms/tellpress

3   Create queries   97

What do you think of this book? We want to hear from you!

Microsoft is interested in hearing your feedback so we can improve our books and learning resources for you. To participate in a brief survey, please visit:

https://aka.ms/tellpress

Introduction

The Microsoft Office Specialist (MOS) certification program has been designed to validate your knowledge of and ability to use programs in the Microsoft Office 2016 suite of programs. This book has been designed to guide you in studying the types of tasks you are likely to be required to demonstrate in Exam 77-730, "Access 2016: Core Database Management, Manipulation, and Query Skills."

Who this book is for

MOS 2016 Study Guide for Microsoft Access is designed for experienced computer users seeking Microsoft Office Specialist certification in Access 2016.

MOS exams for individual programs are practical rather than theoretical. You must demonstrate that you can complete certain tasks or projects rather than simply answer questions about program features. The successful MOS certification candidate will have at least six months of experience using all aspects of the program on a regular basis; for example, using Access at work or school to create and manage databases, build database tables, import and export data, design and run queries, create and format forms, and design detail and summary reports.

As a certification candidate, you probably have a lot of experience with the program you want to become certified in. Many of the procedures described in this book will be familiar to you; others might not be. Read through each study section and ensure that you are familiar with the procedures, concepts, and tools discussed. In some cases, images depict the tools you will use to perform procedures related to the skill set. Study the images and ensure that you are familiar with the options available for each tool.

How this book is organized

The exam coverage is divided into chapters representing broad skill sets that correlate to the functional groups covered by the exam. Each chapter is divided into sections addressing groups of related skills that correlate to the exam objectives. Each section includes review information, generic procedures, and practice tasks you can complete on your own while studying. We provide practice files you can use to work through the practice tasks and result files you can use to check your work. You can practice the generic procedures in this book by using the practice files supplied or by using your own files.

Throughout this book, you will find Exam Strategy tips that present information about the scope of study that is necessary to ensure that you achieve mastery of a skill set and are successful in your certification effort.

Download the practice files

Before you can complete the practice tasks in this book, you need to copy the book's practice files and result files to your computer. Download the compressed (zipped) folder from the following page, and extract the files from it to a folder (such as your Documents folder) on your computer:

https://aka.ms/MOSAccess2016/downloads

IMPORTANT The Access 2016 program is not available from this website. You should purchase and install that program before using this book.

You will save the completed versions of practice files that you modify while working through the practice tasks in this book. If you later want to repeat the practice tasks, you can download the original practice files again.

The following table lists the practice files provided for this book.

Folder and objective group	Practice files	Result files
MOSAccess2016\Objective1 Create and manage databases	Access_1-1.xlsx Access_1-2.accdb Access_1-3.accdb Access_1-4.accdb Access_1-5.accdb	Access_1-1_results.accdb Access_1-2_results.accdb Access_1-3_results.accdb Access_1-4_results.accdb Access_1-5_results.accdb
MOSAccess2016\Objective2 Build tables	Access_2-1a.accdb Access_2-1b.accdb Access_2-1c.txt Access_2-1d.accdb Access_2-2.accdb Access_2-3a.accdb Access_2-3b.xlsx Access_2-4.accdb	Access_2-1_results.accdb Access_2-2_results.accdb Access_2-3_results.accdb Access_2-4_results.accdb
MOSAccess2016\Objective3 Create queries	Access_3-1.accdb Access_3-2.accdb Access_3-3.accdb	Access_3-1_results.accdb Access_3-2_results.accdb Access_3-3_results.accdb
MOSAccess2016\Objective4 Create forms	Access_4-1.accdb Access_4-2.accdb Access_4-3.accdb Access_4-3a.png	Access_4-1_results.accdb Access_4-2_results.accdb Access_4-3_results.accdb
MOSAccess2016\Objective5 Create reports	Access_5-1.accdb Access_5-2.accdb Access_5-3.accdb	Access_5-1_results.accdb Access_5-2_results.accdb Access_5-3_results.accdb

Adapt procedure steps

This book contains many images of user interface elements that you'll work with while performing tasks in Access on a Windows computer. Depending on your screen resolution or program window width, the Access ribbon on your screen might look different from that shown in this book. (If you turn on Touch mode, the ribbon displays significantly fewer commands than in Mouse mode.) As a result, procedural instructions that involve the ribbon might require a little adaptation.

Simple procedural instructions use this format:

➜ On the **Home** tab, in the **Sort & Filter** group, click the **Filter** button.

If the command is in a list, our instructions use this format:

➜ On the **Home** tab, in the **Sort & Filter** group, click **Advanced Filter Options** and then, in the **Advanced Filter Options** list, click **Filter By Form**.

If differences between your display settings and ours cause a button to appear differently on your screen from how it does in this book, you can easily adapt the steps to locate the command. First click the specified tab, and then locate the specified group. If a group has been collapsed into a group list or under a group button, click the list or button to display the group's commands. If you can't immediately identify the button you want, point to likely candidates to display their names in ScreenTips.

The instructions in this book assume that you're interacting with on-screen elements on your computer by clicking (with a mouse, touchpad, or other hardware device). If you're using a different method—for example, if your computer has a touchscreen interface and you're tapping the screen (with your finger or a stylus)—substitute the applicable tapping action when you interact with a user interface element.

Instructions in this book refer to user interface elements that you click or tap on the screen as buttons, and to physical buttons that you press on a keyboard as keys, to conform to the standard terminology used in documentation for these products.

Ebook edition

If you're reading the ebook edition of this book, you can do the following:

- Search the full text
- Print
- Copy and paste

You can purchase and download the ebook edition from the Microsoft Press Store at:

https://aka.ms/MOSAccess2016/detail

Errata, updates, & book support

We've made every effort to ensure the accuracy of this book and its companion content. If you discover an error, please submit it to us through the link at:

https://aka.ms/MOSAccess2016/errata

If you need to contact the Microsoft Press Book Support team, please send an email message to:

mspinput@microsoft.com

For help with Microsoft software and hardware, go to:

https://support.microsoft.com

We want to hear from you

At Microsoft Press, your satisfaction is our top priority, and your feedback our most valuable asset. Please tell us what you think of this book by completing the survey at:

https://aka.ms/tellpress

The survey is short, and we read every one of your comments and ideas. Thanks in advance for your input!

Stay in touch

Let's keep the conversation going! We're on Twitter at:

https://twitter.com/MicrosoftPress

Taking a Microsoft Office Specialist exam

Desktop computing proficiency is increasingly important in today's business world. When screening, hiring, and training employees, employers can feel reassured by relying on the objectivity and consistency of technology certification to ensure the competence of their workforce. As an employee or job seeker, you can use technology certification to prove that you already have the skills you need to succeed, saving current and future employers the time and expense of training you.

Microsoft Office Specialist certification

Microsoft Office Specialist certification is designed to assist students and information workers in validating their skills with Office programs. The following certification paths are available:

- A Microsoft Office Specialist (MOS) is an individual who has demonstrated proficiency by passing a certification exam in one or more Office programs, including Microsoft Word, Excel, PowerPoint, Outlook, or Access.

- A Microsoft Office Specialist Expert (MOS Expert) is an individual who has taken his or her knowledge of Office to the next level and has demonstrated by passing Core and Expert certification exams that he or she has mastered the more advanced features of Word or Excel.

- A Microsoft Office Specialist Master (MOS Master) is an individual who has demonstrated a broader knowledge of Office skills by passing the Word Core and Expert exams, the Excel Core and Expert exams, the PowerPoint exam, and the Access or Outlook exam.

Selecting a certification path

When deciding which certifications you would like to pursue, assess the following:

- The program and program version(s) with which you are familiar
- The length of time you have used the program and how frequently you use it
- Whether you have had formal or informal training in the use of that program
- Whether you use most or all of the available program features
- Whether you are considered a go-to resource by business associates, friends, and family members who have difficulty with the program

Candidates for MOS certification are expected to successfully complete a wide range of standard business tasks. Successful candidates generally have six or more months of experience with the specific Office program, including either formal, instructor-led training or self-study using MOS-approved books, guides, or interactive computer-based materials.

Candidates for MOS Expert and MOS Master certification are expected to successfully complete more complex tasks that involve using the advanced functionality of the program. Successful candidates generally have at least six months, and might have several years, of experience with the programs, including formal, instructor-led training or self-study using MOS-approved materials.

Test-taking tips

Every MOS certification exam is developed from a set of exam skill standards (referred to as the *objective domain*) that are derived from studies of how the Office programs are used in the workplace. Because these skill standards dictate the scope of each exam, they provide critical information about how to prepare for certification. This book follows the structure of the published exam objectives.

See Also For more information about the book structure, see "How this book is organized" in the introduction.

The MOS certification exams are performance based and require you to complete business-related tasks in the program for which you are seeking certification. For example, you might be presented with a document and told to insert and format additional document elements. Your score on the exam reflects how many of the requested tasks you complete within the allotted time.

Here is some helpful information about taking the exam:

- Keep track of the time. Your exam time does not officially begin until after you finish reading the instructions provided at the beginning of the exam. During the exam, the amount of time remaining is shown in the exam instruction window. You can't pause the exam after you start it.

- Pace yourself. At the beginning of the exam, you will receive information about the tasks that are included in the exam. During the exam, the number of completed and remaining tasks is shown in the exam instruction window.

- Read the exam instructions carefully before beginning. Follow all the instructions provided completely and accurately.

- If you have difficulty performing a task, you can restart it without affecting the result of any completed tasks, or you can skip the task and come back to it after you finish the other tasks on the exam.

- Enter requested information as it appears in the instructions, but without duplicating the formatting unless you are specifically instructed to do so. For example, the text and values you are asked to enter might appear in the instructions in bold and underlined text, but you should enter the information without applying these formats.

- Close all dialog boxes before proceeding to the next exam item unless you are specifically instructed not to do so.

- Don't close task panes before proceeding to the next exam item unless you are specifically instructed to do so.

- If you are asked to print a document, worksheet, chart, report, or slide, perform the task, but be aware that nothing will actually be printed.

- Don't worry about extra keystrokes or mouse clicks. Your work is scored based on its result, not on the method you use to achieve that result (unless a specific method is indicated in the instructions).

- If a computer problem occurs during the exam (for example, if the exam does not respond or the mouse no longer functions) or if a power outage occurs, contact a testing center administrator immediately. The administrator will restart the computer and return the exam to the point where the interruption occurred, with your score intact.

Exam Strategy This book includes special tips for effectively studying for the Microsoft Office Specialist exams in Exam Strategy paragraphs such as this one.

Certification benefits

At the conclusion of the exam, you will receive a score report, indicating whether you passed the exam. If your score meets or exceeds the passing standard (the minimum required score), you will be contacted by email by the Microsoft Certification Program team. The email message you receive will include your Microsoft Certification ID and links to online resources, including the Microsoft Certified Professional site. On this site, you can download or order a printed certificate, create a virtual business card, order an ID card, review and share your certification transcript, access the Logo Builder, and access other useful and interesting resources, including special offers from Microsoft and affiliated companies.

Depending on the level of certification you achieve, you will qualify to display one of three logos on your business card and other personal promotional materials. These logos attest to the fact that you are proficient in the applications or cross-application skills necessary to achieve the certification. Using the Logo Builder, you can create a personalized certification logo that includes the MOS logo and the specific programs in which you have achieved certification. If you achieve MOS certification in multiple programs, you can include multiple certifications in one logo.

For more information

To learn more about the Microsoft Office Specialist exams and related courseware, visit:

http://www.certiport.com/mos

 Microsoft Office Specialist

Exam 77-730

Access 2016: Core Database Management, Manipulation, and Query Skills

This book covers the skills you need to have for certification as a Microsoft Office Specialist in Access 2016. Specifically, you need to be able to complete tasks that demonstrate the following skills:

1 Create and manage databases
2 Build tables
3 Create queries
4 Create forms
5 Create reports

With these skills, you can create, populate, and manage the types of databases most commonly used in a business environment.

Prerequisites

We assume that you have been working with Access 2016 for at least six months and that you know how to carry out fundamental tasks that are not specifically mentioned in the objectives for this Microsoft Office Specialist exam.

The certification exam and the content of this book address the processes of designing and building Access databases. We assume that you are familiar with the Microsoft Office ribbon and that you understand basic Access features—for example, that you know how to enter and edit data. We also assume you are familiar with the definition and function of relational databases and database objects such as tables and forms. To provide context and an opportunity for review, the following list provides brief explanations of five important terms:

- **Table** Defines the data stored in a database. Tables are composed of fields, and each field is defined as a specific data type (text, number, date, or another data type). Each field also has certain properties. For example, you can specify that a field is required. You can also define the size of a field (such as the maximum number of characters a field can contain). Users of a database fill in fields (and must fill in required fields) with values to create a record in the database. In most tables, each record is identified by a unique value called a *primary key*, which might be a single field (such as a product ID) or a combination of fields.

- **Relationship** Helps maintain the integrity of the information in a database and reduce data redundancy. You can create several types of relationships between tables in an Access database. In a one-to-many relationship, a record in one table can be related to one or many records in another. You can also create one-to-one relationships and many-to-many relationships. Relationships are created by linking a table's foreign key (such as a customer ID field in an order table) with another table's primary key (the customer ID field in the customer table). Relationships protect data integrity by preventing you from creating orphan records (for example, an order with no customer). Relationships help reduce data redundancy by letting you store information in separate tables that you link together. For example, you can create a customer table and then relate each order in an order table to the record for a specific customer. This prevents you from having to enter a custom record for each separate order.

- **Query** Can be used to select records that meet specific criteria and to perform actions such as updating a group of records. To build a select query, you add fields from one or more tables and then define criteria that Access uses to retrieve the records you want to view. For example, you might want to retrieve records with a certain value in a date field (all records created after 1/1/2017, for example) or records associated with a specific project. Using criteria, you can also create and run action queries that insert, update, or delete selected records.

- **Form** Used to display, enter, and edit data. Forms are often bound to tables (or to queries) that serve as the form's record source. Forms use controls such as text boxes, check boxes, and list boxes to provide a user interface for a database. Forms can also be used to confirm and execute database operations and to navigate from one database object to another. Access provides several built-in form designs, a gallery of form controls, and tools you use to design and lay out a form.

- **Report** Used to share and present data and to summarize data for a specific field or fields. You might print reports for a meeting or distribute them electronically as PDF files or in email.

Objective group 1
Create and manage databases

The skills tested in this section of the Microsoft Office Specialist exam for Microsoft Access 2016 relate to creating and managing databases. Specifically, the following objectives are associated with this set of skills:

1.1   Create and modify databases

1.2   Manage relationships and keys

1.3   Navigate through a database

1.4   Protect and maintain databases

1.5   Print and export data

Many of the operations and tasks involved in creating and managing Access databases originate in the Backstage view. For example, the New page includes templates that you can use to create a database, and a search box that you can use to locate other templates. The Info page provides commands that help you maintain and protect a database. Beyond the specific commands you use, Access also offers a way to back up a database, which is a critical step in ensuring that data is available in the event of an accident or a security incident. By taking steps to make database navigation clear and logical, you help ensure that the database's users have an easy time keeping the data current.

This chapter guides you in studying ways to create and modify databases, manage relationships and keys, navigate through a database, protect and maintain a database, and print and export data.

> To complete the practice tasks in this chapter, you need the practice files contained in the **MOSAccess2016\Objective1** practice file folder. For more information, see "Download the practice files" in this book's introduction.

Objective 1.1: Create and modify databases

When you start Access without opening a recently used database or double-clicking a database file, the program opens to its startup screen. The startup screen displays a list of recent files and a set of thumbnails for templates on which you can base a variety of desktop databases or Access web apps (a type of database stored in the cloud). Access also provides an option for creating a blank desktop database or a custom (blank) web app.

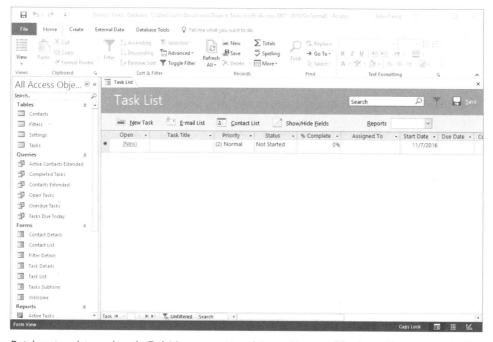

Database templates such as the Task Management template provide a set of database objects you can build on

This topic provides details about how to create a blank desktop database, how to create a database from a template, how to import data to build a database, and how to delete a database object.

Tip On the General page of the Access Options dialog box, you can set options for the default file format for a blank database and the default database folder.

Create databases

Access databases are made up of database objects: tables, queries, forms, reports, and supporting objects such as macros. Templates provide some or all of the database objects you need to manage the type of data the template is designed to support.

When you create a blank database, Access provides a single table by default. You can set up and define other database objects to expand the databases you create. By default, Access names new database files by using Database*n*, where *n* is a number such as 1 or 2. You can enter a more descriptive name when you create the database.

Access provides templates for desktop databases and for what Access calls *SharePoint web apps*. (The thumbnails for web apps display a globe.) When you work with an Access web app, you work in a web browser, but you design and modify the web app in Access. You can share the data in a web app by using an instance of SharePoint.

Exam Strategy Exam 77-730, "Access 2016: Core Database Management, Manipulation, and Query Skills," does not require you to demonstrate that you can create an Access web app.

A blank desktop database opens with the Navigation Pane open. In a blank database, Access creates a default table, called *Table1*, which serves as a starting point. Access displays the default Table1 in what Access refers to as *Datasheet view*. When a table is displayed in Datasheet view, you can define field names and data types and insert records. You can also display a table in *Design view*. In Design view, you work directly with the structure of the table (the table's field names and properties) instead of with the records stored in the table.

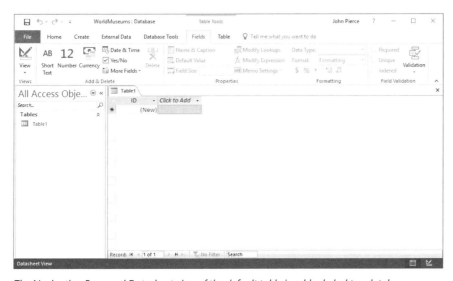

The Navigation Pane and Datasheet view of the default table in a blank desktop database

See Also For more information about how to display objects in the Navigation Pane, see "Display objects in the Navigation Pane" in "Objective 1.3: Navigate through a database."

The database templates represented by the set of thumbnails that appears on the startup page are not the only database templates you can use. At the top of the startup window is the search box, with the prompt "Search for online templates," and just below the search box are suggested search terms. You can search by using one of the suggestions or enter the search term you want to use in the search box to locate other templates that might be available.

When you select a thumbnail for a database template on the startup screen, Access displays a window that provides a description of the template.

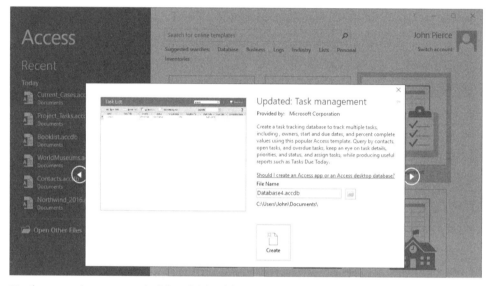

Use the arrows that appear to the left and right of this window to browse through the set of templates

In most cases, when the new database opens, Access displays a table or opens a form for data input. Other objects in the database appear in the Navigation Pane. The Task Management desktop template, for example, includes tables that define records for contacts and tasks. This template also includes several queries used to analyze the data, forms for working with tasks and contacts, and several reports.

Tip Access 2016 includes the Northwind Traders sample database, which has been part of Access for many versions of the program. The Northwind Traders database provides examples of features, including a login dialog box, sample macros, and Microsoft Visual Basic for Application (VBA) modules. Use the search box to find the Northwind Traders database template (the thumbnail identifies the database as *Northwind 2007 sample*). Create the database, and then refer to it when you're looking for a solution, or just work with it from time to time to gain an understanding of the extent of the work you can do in Access.

To create a database from a template

1. On the startup screen or the **New** page of the Backstage view, click the thumb-nail for the template you want to use.

Tip Use the search box to locate a template that's not displayed. To create a blank desktop database, click the Blank Desktop Database thumbnail. (Depending on your installation of Access, the template might be named *Blank Database* or *Blank Desktop Database*.)

---

2. In the **File Name** box, enter a name for the database.

3. If you want to store the database in a location other than your Documents folder, do the following:

    a. Click the folder icon to the right of the **File Name** box.

    b. In the **File New Database** dialog box, navigate to the folder where you want to store the database.

    c. Click **OK**.

4. Click **Create**. Access downloads the template if necessary, and then creates and opens the new database.

5. If an Info bar below the ribbon displays a security warning, click **Enable Content**.

Import database objects and data

Whether you start with a blank database or base your database on a template, you can add some or all of your records by importing data. You can also define part of the structure of the data by, for example, using column headings in a spreadsheet as field names in a new table. Data sources you can use include Excel workbooks, other Access databases, text files, XML files, Microsoft SharePoint lists, and Microsoft Outlook folders.

When you import data, you generally have three options: importing the source data into a new table, appending the data to a table that's already defined, or linking to the data source to create a linked table. When you are importing objects and data as part of creating a database, you use the first of these options in most cases. Access often provides wizards that help you provide the information Access requires to import data from a specific format.

See Also For information about appending data to a table, see "Append records from external data," in "Objective 2.3: Manage records in tables." For information about creating linked tables, see "Create linked tables," in "Objective 2.1: Create tables."

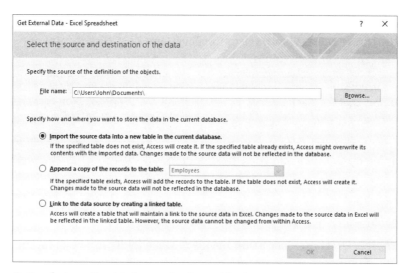

Options for importing data from an Excel spreadsheet

When you import data from Excel into a new table, the Import Spreadsheet Wizard prompts you for information to complete the operation. The wizard first prompts you for the worksheet or the named range you want to import. You can view the sample data that the wizard displays from the worksheet, but you cannot modify it. Access can use the column headings in the worksheet as field names in the database. You can also specify each field's data type and whether Access should index the field. The wizard's fourth page provides options for setting the table's primary key. Access can create an ID field in the table to use as the primary key, or you can select a primary key field or use no primary key in the new table.

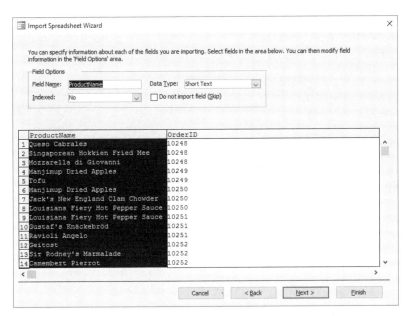

Define field names and data types when you import data from a spreadsheet

See Also For information about running saved import and export operations, see "Objective 1.5: Print and export data."

When you import data from another Access database, you can import all the objects in that database or only the objects you select. The Import Objects dialog box shows the tables, queries, forms, reports, macros, and modules in the source database on separate tabs.

Import options control how the data is imported

The available import options are described in the following list:

- In the Import area, the Relationships option determines whether table relationships are preserved in the import operation. Selecting the Menus And Toolbars option imports any custom menus and toolbars from databases created in versions of Access prior to Access 2007. Selecting Import/Export Specs includes any import or export specifications defined in the source database. Selecting Nav Pane Groups imports any custom Navigation Pane groups set up in the source database, and selecting All Images And Themes includes these elements with the import.

- Options in the Import Tables area control whether you import only the definition of the database objects you select or both the definition of the object and the data. For example, you can import a table with its fields and other properties but no data or include the data in the table. If you are importing objects to create a new database, you might want to import only the definition for a table in which you store project details, but you might want to include the data when you import a table that stores a set of tasks that is common to all projects.

- The options in the Import Queries area determine whether Access imports a query as a query or as a table. You might import a query as a table when the query's definition (the fields it includes) forms the basis of a table you want in a new database.

You can import data from a text file that uses the .txt, .csv, .tab, or .asc file name extension. When you import data from a text file, you work with the Import Text wizard. In the wizard, you first need to specify whether a character separates the fields of data in the text file (a delimited text file) or whether the data is arranged in fixed-width columns. For delimited text files, you need to specify which character is used as the delimiter; for fixed-width files, you indicate where column breaks should occur.

The later pages of the Import Text wizard are similar to those you work with in the Import Spreadsheet wizard. You can name fields, specify a data type, indicate whether the field should be indexed, and skip a specific field. The wizard also prompts you to set up a primary key for the table.

Three of the other formats you can import are as follows:

- **XML files** Access uses the structure of the XML file to determine table names and fields. Import options include Structure Only, Structure And Data, and Append Data To Existing Table(s).

- **SharePoint lists** You provide the URL for the SharePoint site, and you might need to provide your user name and password to gain access to the site. If Access connects to the site successfully, the lists stored on the site are displayed, and you can then select the list or lists that contain the data you want to import. If you select more than one list, each list is imported as a separate table. Access uses the list's name for the table name and the list's columns as the table's fields.

- **Outlook folders** Importing a contacts or tasks folder from Outlook is an effective way to add this information to a database. Access runs the Import Exchange/Outlook wizard when you import data from Outlook. The wizard prompts you to provide field names, specify data types, and set up indexes. You can skip fields if you don't want to import them.

To import data from Excel into a new table

1. On the **External Data** tab, in the **Import & Link** group, click **Excel**.

2. In the **Get External Data** dialog box, click **Import the source data into a new table in the current database**, click **Browse** to locate the source file, and then click **OK**.

3. In the **Import Spreadsheet Wizard**, select the worksheet or named range that has the data you want to import.

4. Click **Next**, and then work through the wizard to specify whether the first column of the data includes column headings, set field options, designate a primary key, and name the table.

5. Click **Finish** in the wizard. If you want to save the steps in this operation, in the **Get External Data** dialog box, select **Save import steps**.

To import data from another Access database

1. On the **External Data** tab, in the **Import & Link** group, click **Access**.

2. In the **Get External Data** dialog box, click **Browse** to locate the source database.

3. Click **Import tables, queries, forms, reports, macros, and modules into the current database**, and then click **OK**.

4. In the **Import Objects** dialog box, do either of the following:

   - To import all the objects from the source database, click **Select All**.

   - To import only specific objects from the source database, select objects you want to import.

5. Click **Options**, and then set the options for the import operation:

   - In the **Import** area, click **Relationships** to preserve table relationships defined in the source database.

   - In the **Import Tables** area, click **Definition and Data** or **Definition Only**.

   - If you are importing queries, in the **Import Queries** area, click **As Queries** or **As Tables**.

6. In the **Get External Data** dialog box, do the following:

   a. If you want to save the steps of the operation for reuse, select the **Save import steps** check box and provide a name and optional description for the steps.

   b. Click **Close**.

To import data from a text file into a new table

1. On the **External Data** tab, in the **Import & Link** group, click **Text File**.

2. In the **Get External Data** dialog box, do the following:

   a. Click **Import the source data into a new table in the current database**.

   b. Click **Browse**. Navigate to and select the source file, and then click **OK**.

3. In the **Import Text** wizard, do the following:

  a. Specify the format for the file you're importing (**Delimited** or **Fixed Width**), and then click **Next**.

  b. Choose the delimiting character or specify column breaks (depending on the format selected in step a). Select **First Row Contains Field Names** if this option applies.

  c. Click **Next**, and then work through the remaining pages to set field options, designate a primary key, and name the table.

  d. In the **Import Text** wizard, click **Finish**.

4. In the **Get External Data** dialog box, do the following:

  a. If you want to save the steps of the operation for reuse, select the **Save import steps** check box and provide a name and optional description for the steps.

  b. Click **Close**.

To import an XML file

1. On the **External Data** tab, in the **Import & Link** group, click **XML**.

2. In the **Get External Data** dialog box, do the following:

  a. Click **Browse** to open the File Open dialog box. Locate and select the source file, and then click **Open**.

  b. Click **OK** to open the Import XML dialog box.

3. In the **Import Options** area of the **Import XML** dialog box, do either of the following, and then click **OK**:

  • To import only the XML file structure as the table's definition, select **Structure Only**.

  • To import the XML file structure and the data values, select **Structure and Data**.

4. In the **Get External Data** dialog box, do the following:

  a. If you want to save the steps of the operation for reuse, select the **Save import steps** check box and provide a name and optional description for the steps.

  b. Click **Close**.

To import a SharePoint list

1. On the **External Data** tab, in the **Import & Link** group, click **More**, and then click **SharePoint List**.

2. In the **Get External Data** dialog box, do the following:

   a. In the **Specify a SharePoint site** box, enter the URL for the SharePoint site you want to connect to.

   b. Click **Import the source data into a new table in the current database**, and then click **Next**.

3. On the **Import data from list** page, for each list that you want to import as a table, do the following:

   a. Select the list check box.

   b. In the **Items to Import** list, select **All Pages** or an option such as **Recent Changes**.

   c. Click **OK**.

4. In the **Get External Data** dialog box, do the following:

   a. If you want to save the steps of the operation for reuse, select the **Save import steps** check box and provide a name and optional description for the steps.

   b. Click **Close**.

To import an Outlook folder as a table

1. On the **External Data** tab, in the **Import & Link** group, click **More**, and then click **Outlook Folder**.

2. In the **Get External Data** dialog box, click **Import the source data into a new table in the current database**, and then click **OK**.

3. If multiple mail profiles are configured on your computer, the Choose Profile dialog box opens. In the dialog box, select the profile you want to import from, and then click **OK**.

4. If prompted, enter the user name and password for your Outlook account.

5. In the **Import Exchange/Outlook Wizard**, do the following:

   a. Select the folder you want to import, and then click **Next**.

   b. Make changes to the field names or data types Access assigns to the folder's contents, set the **Indexed** property for a field, or specify to skip a field. Then click **Next**.

    c. Choose an option to have Access set a primary key, select your own key, or set no primary key. Then click **Next**.

    d. Change the name of the table if you want to, and then click **Finish**.

6. In the **Get External Data** dialog box, do the following:

    a. If you want to save the steps of the operation for reuse, select the **Save import steps** check box and provide a name and optional description for the steps.

    b. Click **Close**.

Delete database objects

Access databases depend on the relationship between tables to preserve the integrity of data and to eliminate redundant data. You can delete most types of database objects, including queries, forms, and reports, without affecting underlying relationships. However, Access prevents you from deleting a table that is related to another table without first deleting the relationship. Access deletes the relationship for you if you agree.

A warning about deleting a table

See Also For more information about table relationships, see "Objective 1.2: Manage relationships and keys." For information about renaming database objects, see "Back up and restore databases" in "Objective 1.4: Protect and maintain databases."

To delete a database object

1. Close the object that you want to delete.

2. In the **Navigation Pane**, right-click the object, and then click **Delete**.

3. In the **Microsoft Access** message box asking you to confirm that you want to delete the object and remove it from all groups, click **Yes**.

4. If you are deleting a table and Access prompts you to confirm that you want Access to delete the relationship, click **Yes** to remove the relationship and delete the table.

Objective 1.1 practice tasks

The practice file for these tasks is located in the **MOSAccess2016\Objective1** practice file folder. The folder also contains a result file that you can use to check your work.

➤ Start Access and do the following:

- ❏ Create a database from the *Desktop contacts* template. (Depending on your installation of Access, the template might be named *Contacts desktop*.) Name the database <u>MOSContacts</u> and save it in the practice file folder.

➤ If you want to explore the contact management database features, play the *Using the Contacts Database* video from the Welcome screen.

Tip If the Welcome screen doesn't open automatically, double-click the Welcome form in the Navigation Pane.

- ❏ Close the MOSContacts database without exiting Access.

➤ From the Access Start screen or the New page of the Backstage view, do the following:

- ❏ From the search box, locate the *Northwind 2007 sample* template.
- ❏ Create a database from the template. Name the database <u>Northwind</u> and save it in the practice file folder.
- ❏ Close the Northwind database without exiting Access.

➤ From the Access Start screen or the New page of the Backstage view, do the following:

- ❏ Create a blank desktop database. (Depending on your installation of Access, the template might be named *Blank database* or *Blank desktop database*.) Name the database <u>MOSDatabase</u> and save it in the practice file folder.
- ❏ Import the Customers and Orders table definitions (not the data) from the Northwind database you created.

Tip Display the Options area and, in the Import Tables section, select Definition Only.

❑ Import the **ExpensesPaid** worksheet from the **Access_1-1** workbook located in the practice file folder to create a new table in the MOSDatabase database, using the worksheet's column headings. Use the ExpenseID field as the primary key. Name the table <u>Expenses</u>.

➤ Open the **Access_1-1_results** database. Compare the two databases to check your work. Then close the open databases.

Objective 1.2: Manage relationships and keys

Formally, Access is known as a *relational database management system*, or RDBMS. In this model, relationships between tables maintain the integrity of the data and reduce the need to store redundant data. For example, customer names can be stored in one table and orders stored in another. By creating a relationship between these tables, you relate each order to a customer; you don't need to repeat the customer's name in the record for new orders. Relationships between tables are also used when you base a query, form, or report on more than one table.

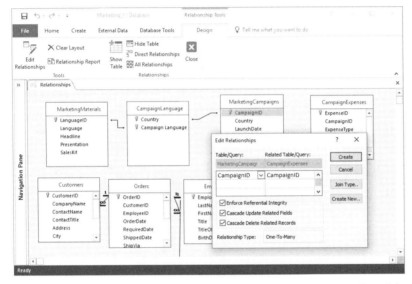

Set options for a relationship in the Relationships window and the Edit Relationships dialog box

This topic describes how to create table relationships, how to set primary keys and foreign keys in an Access database, and how to display relationships in the Relationships window.

Create and modify relationships

When you create a table relationship, the type of the relationship depends on the data that the tables contain and how that data is related. Tables can have the following types of relationships:

- **One-to-many** In this relationship, any one record in the first table can be related to many records in the second table (for example, one customer can place many orders), but any record in the second table (an order) is related to only one record in the first table (for example, each order is placed by a single customer).

- **One-to-one** In a one-to-one relationship, each record in the first table is related to only one record in the second table. You can use a one-to-one relationship to maintain a separate table that defines and stores fields for data that you don't refer to regularly or that you want to keep more confidential. For example, in an Employees table, you can store general employee information such as first and last name, department, job title, and building and office location. In separate EmployeeRating and EmployeeCompensation tables, you can store performance ratings and compensation data—information that you want only certain people or groups to use. Each record in the Employees table has a single matching record in the table for ratings or compensation.

- **Many-to-many** An Orders table and a Products table have a many-to-many relationship because each record in the Orders table can have many matching records in the Products table, and each record in the Products table can have many matching order records. You can't define a many-to-many relationship directly. Instead, you need to create a linking table (also known as a *junction table*) to create two one-to-many relationships. The linking table includes the primary key fields from both the other tables.

Tip In the Northwind sample database that comes with Access, the Order Details table is a linking table.

When you create a relationship, Access displays the Edit Relationships dialog box. If Access detects matching fields in the tables (for example, if each table has a field named CustomerID), Access displays these fields in the Table/Query and Related Table/Query lists. You can replace these default selections when you need to. The relationship type is indicated at the bottom of the dialog box.

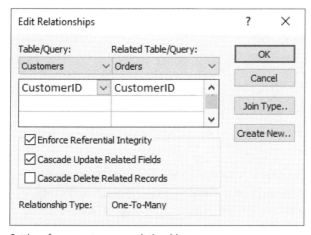

Settings for a one-to-many relationship

See Also For information about join types, see "Create multiple-table queries," in "Objective 3.1: Create queries."

The Edit Relationships dialog box includes several important options, such as the following:

- **Enforce Referential Integrity** Referential integrity is used to prevent orphan records (records in one table with no matching record in a related table) and to maintain references between related tables. By using referential integrity, you ensure that no record in one table refers to a record in another table that doesn't exist; for example, a record for a book cannot refer to an author if a record for that author does not exist. If you enforce referential integrity, Access does not allow operations that violate referential integrity rules for that relationship; for example, you can't enter a customer ID in the Orders table if that customer ID does not exist in the Customers table. Also, you can't delete records that reflect an existing relationship; for example, you can't delete a customer record if order records for that customer exist.

- **Cascade options** When you apply referential integrity to a relationship, you can choose one or both Cascade options:
  - If Cascade Update Related Fields is selected, Access updates the foreign key for all related fields when you make a change to the primary record.
  - If Cascade Delete Related Records is selected, Access deletes all related records when you delete a primary record. If you delete a customer, for example, Access also deletes all order records for that customer.

In a large database with a web of table relationships, you might need to refine the view of the relationships in the Relationships window. You can modify the content of the Relationships window in the following ways:

- Hide a table to remove it from the window.
- Select a set of tables you want to view.
- View the tables with direct relationships for the selected table.
- View all the relationships in the database.
- Drag the table thumbnails to alter the arrangement of the window.

When you close the Relationships window, Access prompts you to save the current layout.

The Object Dependencies pane provides information about how one database object depends on others and how others depend on it. Although the dependencies displayed are not the same as table relationships, you can use the Object Dependencies pane to see, for example, which forms depend on the data or fields in a specific table.

Tip The Relationship Report command in the Tools group on the Relationships Tools Design tool tab produces a printable report of the current layout in the Relationships window.

To open the Relationships window

→ On the **Database Tools** tab, in the **Relationships** group, click **Relationships**.

To display tables in the Relationships window

1. On the **Design** tool tab, in the **Relationships** group, click **Show Table**.

2. In the **Show Table** dialog box, select the tables, and then click **Add**.

Tip Hold down the Ctrl key to select multiple items.

To remove tables from the Relationships window

→ In the **Relationships** window, do either of the following:

- To remove one table, click the table to select it. Then on the **Design** tool tab, in the **Relationships** group, click **Hide Table**.

- To remove all tables, on the **Design** tool tab, in the **Tools** group, click **Clear Layout**.

To display relationships in the Relationships window

→ In the **Relationships** window, do either of the following:

- To display all direct relationships of a specific table, click the table to select it. Then on the **Design** tool tab, in the **Relationships** group, click **Direct Relationships**.

- To display all relationships in the database, on the **Design** tool tab, in the **Relationships** group, click **All Relationships**.

To view object dependencies

1. In the **Navigation Pane**, select the database object whose dependencies you want to view.

2. On the **Database Tools** tab, in the **Relationships** group, click **Object Dependencies**.

3. In the message box informing you that Access needs to update dependency information, click **OK**.

4. In the **Object Dependencies** pane, click **Objects that depend on me** or **Objects that I depend on**.

To create a table relationship

1. Open the **Relationships** window. If the tables you want to create relationships between aren't displayed in the Relationships window, add them.

2. Drag the linking field from the first table (the "one" table in a one-to-many relationship) to the second table (the "many" table).

3. In the **Edit Relationships** dialog box that opens, do the following:

   a. Ensure that the linking fields are selected in the **Table/Query** and **Related Table/Query** lists.

   b. If you want to enforce referential integrity for this relationship, select the **Enforce Referential Integrity** check box.

   c. If you enforce referential integrity, you can also do one or both of the following:

      ○ If you want Access to update related fields when you change the primary record, select the **Cascade Update Related Fields** check box.

      ○ If you want Access to delete related records when you delete the primary record, select the **Cascade Delete Related Records** check box.

   d. Click **Create** to establish the relationship and close the dialog box.

To modify a relationship

1. Open the **Relationships** window and do either of the following:

   • Click the relationship line between two tables. Then on the **Design** tool tab, in the **Tools** group, click **Edit Relationship**.

   • Right-click the relationship line between two tables, and then click **Edit Relationship**.

2. In the **Edit Relationships** dialog box, modify the table or query selections, the join type, or the options, and then click **OK**.

Set key fields

In Access, key fields are used when you establish table relationships. For example, if you have a table named *Project Managers*, the table could include the ProjectManagerID field as its *primary key*. A table's primary key uniquely identifies each record in the table. You can then add the ProjectManagerID field to the Projects table to create a relationship between the tables that lets you identify the manager for each project. In the Projects table, the ProjectManagerID field is referred to as a *foreign key*. Primary keys and foreign keys can also be used in queries to join tables; Access uses that relationship to retrieve the set of records that match the criteria you define.

You can use a single field (for example, a unique product or customer code, or an ID field that is set to the AutoNumber data type that Access provides) or a combination of fields as a table's primary key. A multifield primary key is called a *composite key*. For an AutoNumber field, Access assigns a unique number to each record in a table; you don't need to keep track of values that might be duplicates. If you don't use the

AutoNumber data type but instead use a field whose value you enter, be sure that you set the field's Required property to Yes and that you use a field or a combination of fields whose values change infrequently or not at all.

See Also For information about setting field properties, see "Objective 2.4: Create and modify fields."

Tip When you create a new table, Access includes an ID field in the table and sets this field to be the table's primary key.

A foreign key field should be set to the Number data type. You do not need to enter data for the foreign key field. Instead, the field's values are tied to the unique values from the table in which the field is the primary key field.

To set the primary key for a table, you must have the table open in Design view. Access adds a small key icon to the row selector area to indicate that a field is a primary key field.

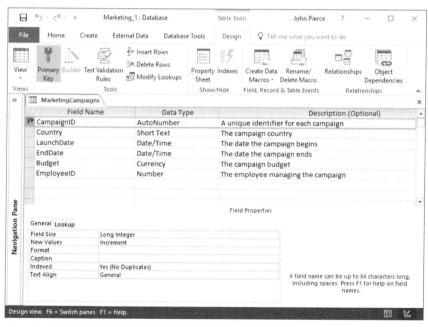

A key icon identifies the primary key field

If a table already contains data, the field or fields you designate for the primary key must have unique values. Also, if a primary key field is part of any table relationship, you must remove the relationship before you can change the primary key.

See Also For information about adding and deleting relationships, see "Create and modify relationships" earlier in this topic.

To open a table in Design view

→ If the table is closed, right-click the table in the **Navigation Pane**, and then click **Design View**.

→ If the table is open in another view, on the **Design** tool tab, in the **Views** group, click **View**, and then click **Design View**.

See Also For more information about object views, see "Change object views" in "Objective 1.3: Navigate through a database."

To set a primary key

1. Open the table in Design view.

2. Select the field or fields you want to designate as the table's primary key. To select multiple fields, press **Ctrl** and select the fields.

3. On the **Design** tool tab, in the **Tools** group, click **Primary Key**.

To remove the primary key designation from a field

1. Open the table in Design view.

2. Select the field or fields from which you want to remove the primary key designation.

3. On the **Design** tool tab, in the **Tools** group, click **Primary Key**.

To set a foreign key in a table

1. Open the table in Design view.

2. In the **Field Name** column, enter the name of the foreign key field.

3. In the **Data Type** column, select **Number**.

4. Save the changes to the table.

Objective 1.2 practice tasks

The practice file for these tasks is located in the **MOSAccess2016\Objective1** practice file folder. The folder also contains a result file that you can use to check your work.

➤ Open the **Access_1-2** database from the practice file folder, and then do the following:

❑ Open the Status table in Design view.

❑ Set the StatusID field as the table's primary key.

❑ Save the changes to the table.

➤ Open the Relationships window and do the following:

❑ Display the Tasks and Status tables in the window.

❑ Create a relationship between the Status table (StatusID field) and the Tasks table (Status field).

❑ Use the Show Table command to add the Compensation table to the Relationships window.

❑ Edit the relationship between the Compensation table and the Employees table to enforce referential integrity.

➤ Open the **Access_1-2_results** database. Compare the two databases to check your work. Then close the open databases.

Objective 1.3: Navigate through a database

In an Access database, navigational features can be different for users who are responsible for designing and maintaining the database and for users whose role is only to enter, edit, and view data. Later in this topic, you examine how to create a navigation form that greets database users when they open a database and provides a set of controls for opening forms, running queries, and viewing and printing reports. In this topic, you also study how to find specific records, set up different views in the Navigation Pane, and work with basic Access views.

Navigate specific records

You have a choice of tools when you need to find a specific record in a table or in the results of a query, or when you're working with a form or report. Navigation buttons that appear at the bottom of a form or a table in Datasheet view move from record to record or to the first or last record. The record indicator displays which record is selected. The navigation area also includes a simple search box in which you can enter the text you want to search for. Access finds the first instance of that text in any of the object's fields.

⊞	36 Mariya Sergienko	Company C
⊞	37 Laura Giussani	Company F
⊞	38 Anne Hellung-Lar	Company BB
⊞	39 Jan Kotas	Company H
⊞	40 Mariya Sergienko	Company J
⊞	41 Nancy Freehafer	Company G ⌄
⊞	42 Nancy Freehafer	Company J
⊞	43 Nancy Freehafer	Company K
⊞	44 Nancy Freehafer	Company A
⊞	45 Nancy Freehafer	Company BB
⊞	46 Robert Zare	Company I
⊞	47 Michael Neipper	Company F
⊞	48 Mariya Sergienko	Company H
⊞	50 Anne Hellung-Lar	Company Y

Record: ◄◄ ◄ 12 of 48 ► ►► ►⁂   ⧩ No Filter   Company G

Datasheet View

Use the search box in the navigation area to find specific records

On the Home tab, commands in the Find group help you locate records, perform find-and-replace operations, and move between records by using the Go To options. In the Find dialog box, you can select an option to search the current field or the current document (the full database). The Match box provides options for matching the whole field, any part of the field, or the start of the field. For example, if you were searching for records for *pasta*, you could enter <u>pasta</u> and match the whole field, <u>pa</u> and match the start of the field, or <u>st</u> and match any part of the field. You can also conduct case-sensitive searches. The Search Fields As Formatted check box is selected by default. You can clear this option to search for values as Access stores them rather than as they are formatted in the database.

Another approach for navigating to a specific record is to use the options that Access provides for sorting and filtering records. You can sort the records in text fields in ascending or descending order, and in number fields from smallest to largest or largest to smallest. When you filter records, only the records that match the filter's criteria are displayed. This reduces a long list of records to just a few records among many.

See Also For information about sorting and filtering records, see "Find, sort, and filter data" in "Objective 2.3: Manage records in tables."

To use the navigation area

→ In the navigation area at the bottom of a table, query, or form, use the arrows to move to the first, next, previous, or last record in the record set.

→ To find a specific record, in the navigation area's search box, enter text related to the record.

To go to a record

→ On the **Home** tab, in the **Find** group, click **Go To**, and then click **First**, **Previous**, **Next**, or **Last**.

To find records

1. On the **Home** tab, in the **Find** group, click **Find**.

2. In the **Find And Replace** dialog box, in the **Find What** box, enter text related to the record you want to locate.

3. Use the **Look In**, **Match**, and **Search** lists and the **Match Case** option to specify conditions that Access will use to locate records.

4. Click **Find Next**.

Create and modify navigation forms

To augment or replace the Navigation Pane, you can build a form that database users use to open forms, run queries, view reports, and perform other database operations.

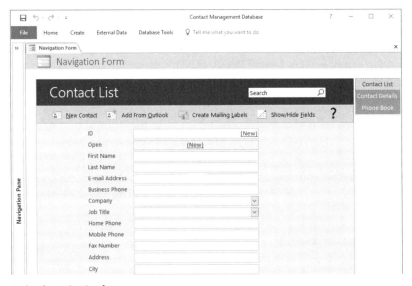

A simple navigation form

Access provides several default layouts for navigation forms. Each of the built-in layouts provides tabs (in various locations and orientations) that users click to display the object they want to use. You can add other forms and reports to the navigation form to complete it. As you add objects to the navigation form's tabs, Access duplicates the Add New tab, to mark where the next object tab will appear. You can also insert a navigation button to add a link in a specific position.

To create a navigation form

1. On the **Create** tab, in the **Forms** group, click **Navigation**, and then click the layout you want to use.

2. Expand the **Navigation Pane** if it is collapsed.

3. Drag the first database object (a form or report, for example) that you want to add to the navigation form from the **Navigation Pane** to the **Add New** area of the navigation form.

4. For each additional object that you want to add to the form, drag the object from the **Navigation Pane** and drop it before or after an existing tab.

5. To create a navigation tab that isn't linked to a specific object, do either of the following:

    - To insert a tab after the existing tabs, double-click the **[Add New]** tab, and then click away from it.

    - To insert a tab between others, right-click the tab that is currently in the position you want for the new tab, and then click **Insert Navigation button**.

6. In the content area of the program window, right-click the form tab, and then click **Save**.

Set a form as the startup option

After you create a navigation form, you can select it as the default form that Access displays when you open the database. You can use this option to designate any form in your database as the default form to display. You don't need to select a navigation form.

To specify a startup form

1. Open the **Access Options** dialog box and display the **Current Database** page.

2. In the **Application Options** section, open the **Display Form** list, and click the form you want to use.

Display objects in the Navigation Pane

This section focuses on the Access Navigation Pane and how you can modify and organize it to display different views of the objects in a database. The ability to modify the Navigation Pane means that it can serve the needs of a range of users—from a database's designer to its casual users.

The Northwind sample database provides examples of how you can configure the Navigation Pane. In the Northwind database, objects by default are arranged within several categories, not by object name or object type. Objects are grouped under headings such as Customers & Orders, Suppliers, and Shippers instead of headings such as Tables, Queries, and Forms. Headings such as Customers & Orders help clarify functional areas of the database and help users find forms and queries related to the area they are working with.

When you change how database objects are displayed in the Navigation Pane, you work with a menu that has several options. This menu arranges commands in two areas, marked by the shaded labels Navigate To Category and Filter By Group. The Navigate To Category area includes categories such as Object Type, Tables And Related Views, Created Date, and Modified Date. For each category, the Filter By

Group area provides options that you can apply to display a subset of objects. For example, if you select Modified Date in the Navigate To Category area, you can then filter the list by selecting Today, Three Weeks Ago, Yesterday, Older, or All Dates. For the Object Type category, you can filter the Navigation Pane to view only objects of a specific type or view all objects.

The Tables And Related Views category displays each table in the database together with other database objects that depend on it. Using this view is helpful when you make changes to a table's design. For example, by choosing the Tables And Related Views category and then choosing a single table in the Filter By Group area, you can see which objects depend on the table, and you can review the design of those objects to be sure that the changes you want to make to the table won't affect the other objects in ways you don't intend.

You can also sort the list of objects in a category, showing them in ascending or descending order or by name, type, and date criteria. You can also change the level of detail that is shown for objects in the Navigation Pane. You can display a list of names with a small icon, show a larger icon next to the name of the object, or show details such as the created and modified date for the object.

The search bar at the top of the Navigation Pane helps you locate a specific object (or group of objects) by name. As you enter a text string, Access filters the list of objects and displays those that match.

As with the Northwind sample database, database templates often provide a specific category for viewing database objects by functional role. For example, the Task Management template provides a category called *Tasks Navigation*, which lets you filter by groups such as tasks and contacts. A blank desktop database includes a category named *Custom* that you can rename and use to build your own Navigation Pane view.

You can set up Navigation Pane categories and groups of your own in the Navigation Options dialog box.

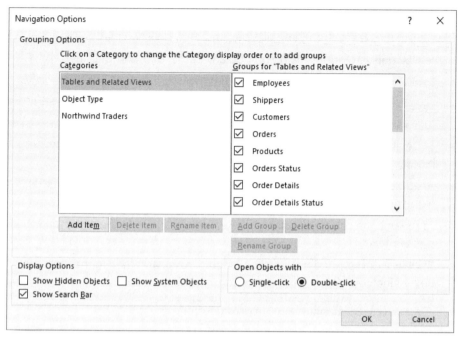

Organize the Navigation Pane into categories and groups

The categories defined for the database appear in the list at the left, and each group defined for a category appears in the list at the right. You can hide a group from being displayed in the Navigation Pane, or select display options to show hidden and system objects in the Navigation Pane or to show or hide the search bar. By using the Open Objects With options, you can control whether an object opens when it is clicked (similar to a hyperlink) or double-clicked.

In the Groups For list is a group named *Unassigned Objects*, which is a built-in group that contains all the objects in a database. When you work with the default Custom category in a blank database, Access also provides a group named *Custom Group 1*.

Tip You can reposition a custom category or group by using the arrows that appear beside an item's name when you select it. You cannot place a custom category above the two built-in categories or place a custom group below the built-in group Unassigned Objects.

When you add a database object to a custom group, you add only a shortcut to that object, not the object itself. This means that you can delete a shortcut from a custom group without deleting the database object.

To create and modify Navigation Pane categories and groups

1. Right-click the **Navigation Pane** title bar, and then click **Navigation Options**.

2. In the **Navigation Options** dialog box, do any of the following, and then click **OK**:

   - To add a category, click **Add Item** and then enter a name for the category.

   - To rename the selected category, click **Rename Item**, edit the name, and then press **Enter**.

   - To delete the selected category, click **Delete Item**, and then in the message box asking you to confirm the deletion, click **OK**.

   - To add a group to the selected category, click **Add Group**, and then enter a name for the group.

   - To rename the selected group, click **Rename Group**, edit the name, and then press **Enter**.

   - To delete the selected group, click **Delete Group**, and then in the message box asking you to confirm the deletion, click **OK**.

     Tip You can rename and delete only custom groups.

   - In the **Display Options** area, select or clear the check boxes for showing hidden objects, system objects, and the search bar.

   - In the **Open Objects With** area, click **Single-click** or **Double-click**.

To add objects to a group

1. In the **Navigation Pane**, display the **Unassigned Objects** group.

2. Right-click the object you want to add to the group, click **Add to group**, and then select the group.

Change object views

You work with database objects in a variety of views. Each type of object (tables, queries, forms, and reports) can be opened in Design view. In Design view, you can add and define fields and field properties for a table; add fields to a query; add command buttons, list boxes, and other controls to a form; and apply formatting, group records, add calculated fields, and complete other tasks when you work with reports.

Forms and reports can also be opened in Layout view. In Layout view, you can design and modify a form or report while viewing the actual data. In Design view, data is not displayed. When you work with a form (for data entry or when searching for a specific record), the form is displayed in Form view. When you view a completed report, the report is displayed in Report view.

When you open a table for data entry or view the results that a query returns, you work with the table or query in Datasheet view.

To change object views

→ In the **Navigation Pane**, right-click the object and then choose the view you want to use. (Not every object view is available on the menu.)

→ With the database object open, right-click the object's tab in the Access design window, and then select the view you want to use.

→ With the database object open, click **View** on the object's **Design** tool tab, and then select the view you want to use. (For tables, the View command appears on the Fields tool tab.)

Objective 1.3 practice tasks

The practice file for these tasks is located in the **MOSAccess2016\Objective1** practice file folder. The folder also contains a result file that you can use to check your work.

➤ Open the **Access_1-3** database from the practice file folder, and then do the following:

  ❑ Open the Customers table in Datasheet view. Use the search box to locate the record for *The Big Cheese*.

  ❑ Create a Navigation Pane category named <u>Campaigns</u>, and groups named <u>Campaign Details</u>, <u>Products</u>, and <u>Employees</u>.

  ❑ Add the Campaign Expenses, CampaignLanguages, and Marketing Campaigns tables to the Campaign Details group. Add the Orders and Products tables to the Products group, and add the Employees table to the Employees group.

  ❑ Create a navigation form that has the Vertical Tabs, Left layout. Add the TaskDetails form to the navigation form. Save the form (use the default name for this practice task), and then set the form as the startup form.

➤ Open the **Access_1-3_results** database. Compare the two databases to check your work. Then close the open databases.

Objective 1.4: Protect and maintain databases

Access provides several options for maintaining and protecting a database. The first of these—Compact & Repair—can help improve the performance of a database and can repair database files in the event of a problem. You can use the Encrypt With Password option to restrict database access to only those users who know the password.

This topic describes these options and other tasks you perform to protect and maintain a database, including backing up a database, recovering data from a backup, and splitting a database—a step that applies especially to a database shared by multiple users.

Compact and repair databases

As you and other users work with an Access database, the database file grows larger as you add data and because Access creates and uses hidden objects to perform its work behind the scenes. Database files can also become corrupt. Frequent use of the database—especially by multiple users working on the database over a network—can result in a corrupted file, which can in some cases result in data loss or affect the ease with which you can change the database's design.

To keep ahead of these potential problems, you can compact and repair a database. You can perform these operations on the current database (the database you have open) or select a different database when you perform these operations.

Some restrictions apply to compacting and repairing a database. For example, if more than one person has the database open when you compact or repair it, Access displays a message indicating that you attempted to open a database that is already open. Before you compact a multiuser database, you should be sure that no one has the database open and then open the database for exclusive access.

Tip Select the Compact On Close option on the Current Database page of the Access Options dialog box to compact a database each time you close it.

To open a database for exclusive access

1. If the database is open, click the **File** tab, and then click **Close**. (If other users have the database open, they must also close the database.)

2. Display the **Open** page of the Backstage view. In the **Places** list, click the location where the database is stored, such as This PC. Then click **Browse**.

3. In the **Open** dialog box, navigate to the folder where the database is stored, and then select the database.

4. Click the **Open** arrow, and then click **Open Exclusive**.

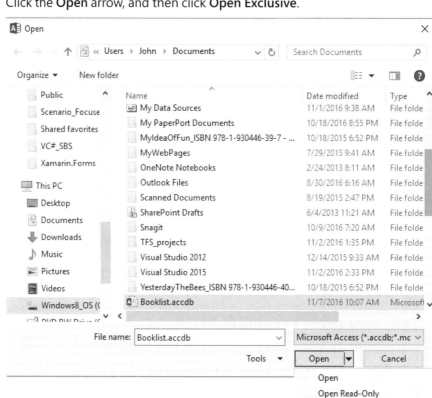

Opening a database for exclusive access

To compact and repair the current database

1. Open the database for exclusive access.

2. On the **Info** page of the Backstage view, click **Compact & Repair Database**.

To compact and repair a database that isn't currently open

1. Close any open databases.

2. On the **Database Tools** tab, in the **Tools** group, click **Compact and Repair Database**.

3. In the **Database to Compact From** dialog box, select the database you want to compact, and then click **Compact**.

4. In the **Compact Database Into** dialog box, enter a name for the compacted database, and then click **Save**.

5. If you used the current name of the database, click **Yes** in the message box Access displays to confirm that Access should replace the current database file.

Back up and restore databases

Another step in protecting your database files from corruption and the potential loss of data is to perform regular backups. In practice, you need to back up some databases more often than others. A database that serves as an archive, for example, and isn't used frequently, doesn't need to be backed up on a specific schedule. A database that you and others work with nearly every day should be backed up on a regular schedule. You should also follow standard backup procedures such as keeping the backup copies on external media (such as a DVD or a flash drive) and in a secure location.

Exam Strategy The objective domain for this exam includes backing up a database and recovering database objects from a backup. You might be required to demonstrate the recovery of specific objects, such as tables.

When you back up a database, Access appends the current date to the name of the database file. You can retain this date or replace it with an alternative identifier. You might also add "backup" to the file name so that you can identify a backup easily.

If one or more objects in a database become corrupt, if you lose data, or if you need to return to an earlier version of a database for some other reason, you can restore a database by replacing it with a backup file. You can also recover specific database objects by importing them from a recent backup.

IMPORTANT You might be able to at least partially repair a corrupt database by running the Compact & Repair command. For information, see "Compact and repair databases" earlier in this topic.

Recovering an object from a backup doesn't automatically replace the original object. For example, if you restore a table named *Tasks* from a recent backup, Access creates a table named *Tasks1* in the current database. Before you begin the steps to recover a database object, you should delete the object from the current database or rename the original object (by adding an identifier such as "old" or "bad").

To back up a database

1. Display the **Save As** page of the Backstage view.

2. In the **Advanced** area, click **Back Up Database**, and then click **Save As**.

3. In the **Save As** dialog box, modify the file name that Access provides (or accept the default name), and then click **Save**.

To rename a database object

1. In the **Navigation Pane**, right-click the object, and then click **Rename** to activate the object name for editing.

2. Enter the new object name, and then press **Enter**.

See Also For information about deleting database objects, see "Delete database objects" in "Objective 1.1: Create and modify databases."

To restore database objects from a backup

1. Open the database in which you want to restore an object.

2. In the **Navigation Pane**, rename or delete the current instance of the object. (If you are restoring a missing object, you can ignore this step.)

3. On the **External Data** tab, in the **Import & Link** group, click **Access**.

4. In the **Get External Data** dialog box, click **Import tables, queries, forms, reports, macros, and modules into the current database**.

5. Click **Browse** and navigate to the backup file you want to use. Then click **Open**.

6. In the **Get External Data** dialog box, click **OK**.

7. In the **Import Objects** dialog box, do either of the following, and then click **OK**:

    - Click **Select All** to select all the objects and restore the entire database.

    - Select the object or objects you want to restore.

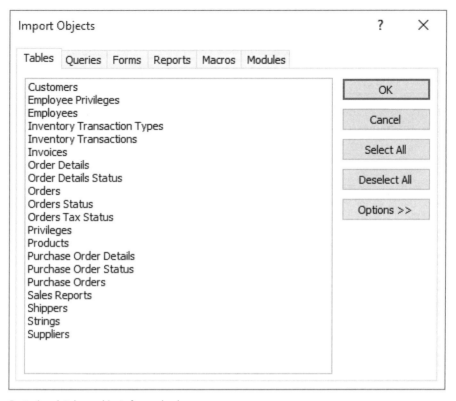

Restoring database objects from a backup

8. In the **Get External Data** dialog box, click **Close**.

Split a database

You can think of an Access database as composed of two parts. The tables, which define and store the raw data, make up one part (the back end). The second part consists of the queries, forms, reports, and supporting objects that users interact with to enter, edit, and view data (the front end). You can split a database to store the tables in one file and the other database objects in a second file. Splitting a database into a front end and back end allows the database designers and administrators to create new forms or update reports for the front end without interfering with the use of the back-end database while doing so. When the new objects are ready, the administrators can implement the updated front end without affecting the relationships and references in place in the back end.

Another reason to split a database is to reduce network traffic when the database is used by more than one person. The back-end database (the tables) can reside in a shared location, and each person can use a local copy of the front-end database.

Tip You should back up your database before you split it.

After you split a database, Access displays a small arrow icon in the Navigation Pane next to the names of tables.

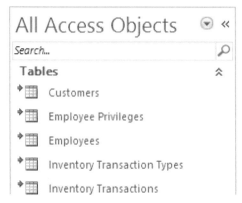

The arrows in the Navigation Pane indicate tables that are linked to the back-end database

To split a database

1. Close all open database objects.

2. On the **Database Tools** tab, in the **Move Data** group, click **Access Database**. If Access displays a security notice that shows the path to the file ACWZTOOL. ACCDE, click **Open** to proceed and open the Database Splitter dialog box.

3. In the **Database Splitter** dialog box, read through the information provided, and then click **Split Database**.

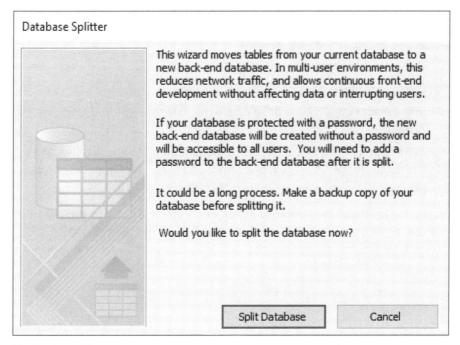

The Database Splitter

4. In the **Create Back-end Database** dialog box, choose a location for the back-end file. By default, Access uses the current database name and adds *_be* to the end of the file name.

5. Click **Split** to begin the process. When the process completes, in the **Database Splitter** message box confirming that the database split was successful, click **OK**.

Encrypt database files

When you assign a password to a database, any user who wants to work with the data-base must enter the password to open the file. You can use this process, for example, to restrict who can open a database that is stored in a location that many users share.

A database must be open for exclusive use before you can encrypt the database by using a password. If you are encrypting the current database, you need to close it before you open it for exclusive use.

IMPORTANT If any properties of the database are incompatible with encryption, Access displays a message box telling you that the feature (such as row-level locking) will be ignored. You can safely dismiss this message and proceed with encryption.

You can also remove a password from a database after you open it for exclusive use.

To encrypt a database with a password

1. Close the database without exiting Access.
2. Display the **Open** page of the Backstage view.
3. In the **Places** list, click the drive where the database is stored, and then click **Browse**.
4. In the **Open** dialog box, navigate to the database storage location and select the database file. Click the **Open** arrow, and then click **Open Exclusive**.
5. On the **Info** page of the Backstage view, click **Encrypt with Password**.
6. In the **Set Database Password** dialog box, enter the password you want to use, enter the password again in the **Verify** box, and then click **OK**.

Enter a password to protect the database

To remove a database password

1. Open the database for exclusive access, and enter the database password.
2. On the **Info** page of the Backstage view, click **Decrypt Database**.
3. In the **Unset Database Password** dialog box, enter the password applied to the database, and then click **OK**.

Objective 1.4 practice tasks

The practice file for these tasks is located in the **MOSAccess2016\Objective1** practice file folder. The folder also contains a result file that you can use to check your work.

➤ Open the **Access_1-4** database from the practice file folder for exclusive use, and then do the following:

- ❏ Log on by using any user name.
- ❏ Create a password for the database. Use the password <u>Access2016</u>.
- ❏ Compact and repair the database.
- ❏ Create a backup of the database. Name the backup <u>MOSBackup</u>.
- ❏ Rename the Customer List form as <u>Customer List_old</u>.
- ❏ Restore the Customer List form from the *MOSBackup* database.
- ❏ Delete the Customer List_old form.
- ❏ Split the **Access_1-4** database to create a front-end database and a back-end database. Save the back-end database in the practice file folder using the default name *Access_1-4_be*.

➤ Open the **Access_1-4_results** database. Compare the two databases to check your work. Then close the open databases.

Objective 1.5: Print and export data

You can use the data you store in Access in several ways. Within Access, you can create reports, for example, and distribute the reports in printed or electronic format. You can also export data to formats that are compatible with earlier versions of Access and with other programs, including Microsoft Excel and Word.

This topic first focuses on how to print reports and specific database records. It then describes how to export data from Access and how to save a database as a template.

Print reports and records

When you print a report, you can send the report directly to the default printer (without setting any printing options), use the Print dialog box to select a printer and set printing options, or work in print preview, a view that enables you to refine the report's layout, view the report in different ways, and export the data.

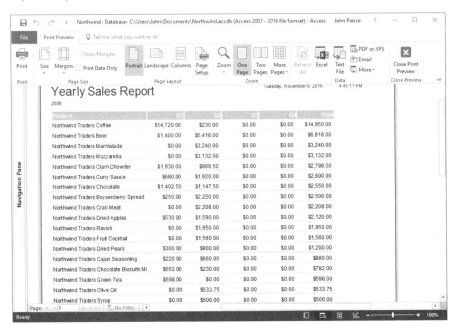

A report open in print preview

The Print dialog box provides standard options with which you can specify a page range, set the number of copies, and adjust the page setup. It also provides an option for printing selected records. You must select the records you want to print before opening the Print dialog box. In general, you will print records that you select in a table or query that is open in Datasheet view.

When you display a report in print preview, Access provides commands to adjust page size and margins, change the page layout and page orientation (switching from portrait to landscape, for example), set up the report in columns, and view the report by zooming in and out or by displaying one or more pages. With these views, you can assess whether the report's formatting is consistent, for example, or whether any important data might be missing. Many of the commands on the Print Preview tab are also available when you design and format a report in Design view or Layout view.

Tip The Print Preview tab also provides a set of options (in the Data group) for exporting data to other programs or in various formats. These options are described in "Export data" later in this topic.

In the Page Size group on the Print Preview tab, the Show Margins option displays or hides the report's margins, and the Print Data Only option removes elements such as column headings and information in page headers and footers from the report that Access prints. You can open the Page Setup dialog box from the Page Size group, but many of the options in the Page Size and Page Layout groups duplicate options that the dialog box provides.

The range of zoom levels in print preview extends from 10 percent to a maximum of 1,000 percent (not all zoom levels apply to every object), but you can choose only preset options (such as 75% or 200%). The Zoom slider, in the lower-right corner of the Access window, adjusts the zoom level with greater flexibility. The Zoom group also lets you choose how many pages to display in a multipage report or printout. By default, one page is displayed. You can also display 2, 4, 8, or 12 pages.

To print a report directly to the default printer

→ Right-click the report, and then click **Print**.

Or

1. Open the report from the **Navigation Pane**.

2. On the **Print** page of the Backstage view, click **Quick Print**.

To set printing options and print a report

1. Open the report from the **Navigation Pane**.

2. On the **Print** page of the Backstage view, click **Print**.

3. In the **Print** dialog box, set options for the print range, number of copies, and other printer properties. Then click **OK**.

To print selected records from a table or a query

1. Open the table or query in Datasheet view.

2. Select the records you want to print.

3. On the **Print** page of the Backstage view, click **Print**.

4. In the **Print** dialog box, do the following:

    a. In the **Print range** area, click **Selected Records**. (If you don't click **Selected Records**, Access prints all the records in the datasheet.)

    b. Click **OK**.

To manage print and page setup options for a database object in print preview

1. Open the database object you want to print, if it is not already open.

2. On the **Print** page of the Backstage view, click **Print Preview**.

3. In the **Page Size** group, adjust paper size and margins and specify whether only data should be printed.

4. In the **Page Layout** group, set the page orientation, columns, and other page setup options.

5. In the **Print** group, click **Print**.

6. In the **Print** dialog box, set options for the number of copies and other printing options, and then click **OK.**

Save a database as a template

As described earlier in this chapter, you can use a template as the basis for a new database. The template can provide a set of default database objects (tables, forms, and reports, for example) that you customize for the needs of a specific database.

You can also save a database that you create (either from scratch or by using a template) as a template. You might use this option to save a basic contact database that includes information you need in more than one database. You might also create a set of forms with a look and feel that you want each database to include and then save those forms as a template. By default, templates are stored in your user profile, in \AppData\Roaming\Microsoft\Templates\Access.

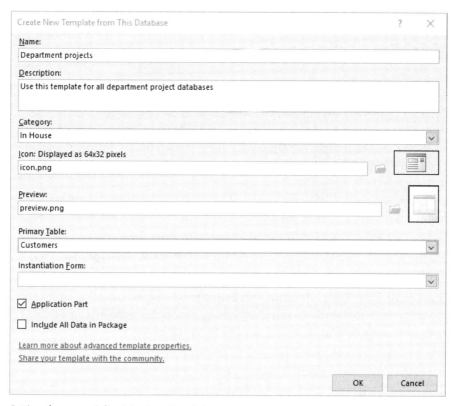

Settings for a user-defined database template

In the Create New Template From This Database dialog box, you can categorize the templates you create. Access sets the Category box to User Templates by default, but you can define a category of your own and assign a template to it. If you plan to share this template with other users or just want to add a professional touch to a template you're creating for yourself, you can specify an image file to use as an icon for the template. This icon replaces the standard Access icon in the program's application window and as the thumbnail preview of the template that appears in the Backstage view. You can also specify a preview image and a form that appears when the database opens. If the database you are saving as a template already includes data, you can include that data in the template or include only the database objects themselves, without any data.

The Instantiation Form list specifies the form you want to display as a splash screen, for example. Access displays the form you select in this list only once and then deletes the form. Be careful not to confuse this option with a startup form, which you can specify for the current database by using the Access Options dialog box.

You can include the template as an application part, which makes it available in the Application Parts gallery on the Create tab. The application part appears under the heading you provide in the Category box in the Create New Template From This Database dialog box. The template is also available on the Access startup screen or on the New page in the Backstage view.

To save a database as a template

1. Create and format the database objects you want to include in the template. Enter any data you want the template to store by default.

2. Click the **File** tab, and then click **Save As**. In the **Database File Types** list, click **Template**, and then click **Save As**.

3. In the **Create New Template from This Database** dialog box, enter a name and description for the database, and then specify a category, icon image, preview image, and instantiation form (if you want to use one).

4. Select the **Application Part** check box to add this template to the Application Parts gallery, and then specify a primary table for the template.

5. Select **Include All Data in Package** as applicable.

Export data

One of the advantages of entering and maintaining data in a database is the capability to make the data available in other formats. For example, you can export data to use it in other programs and in other contexts. Data related to sales, budgets, orders, and other financial records can be exported to Excel for analysis. A list of contacts can be exported to a list in a SharePoint site or used in a mail merge in Word. Exporting data to a text file or to an XML file puts the data in a format that is compatible with other database and spreadsheet programs, and creating a PDF or an XPS file by using an export operation lets you distribute data in formats designed for review instead of analysis and editing.

The Export dialog box provides options to maintain an object's formatting and layout when you export it, view the exported file when the operation is complete, and export only selected records (in lieu of the complete record set that is contained in a specific table or query, for example). Specific operations, such as exporting to a text file, require you to set additional options that control where and how data is exported. You can also save export settings and then repeat an export operation in a single step.

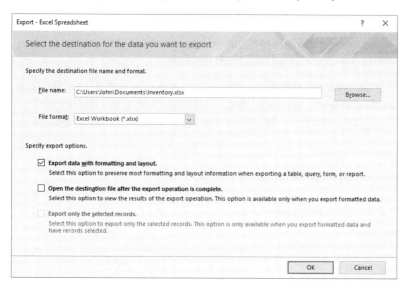

Exporting data to an Excel workbook

The default setting for exporting data to Excel is the Excel Workbook file format (.xlsx). The options you can choose for a file format depend on the type of object you export. When you export records from a query, for example, you can keep Excel Workbook (.xlsx) or choose Excel Binary Workbook, Microsoft Excel 5.0/95 Workbook, or Excel 97–Excel 2003 Workbook. If you export a report, the file formats are limited to Microsoft Excel 5.0/95 Workbook and Excel 97–Excel 2003 Workbook.

The availability of export options also depends on the type of object. If you export a report, the Export Data With Formatting And Layout check box is selected by default and cannot be cleared. If you export a query or a table, you can select or clear the formatting and layout check box. By selecting that check box, you can open the destination file, and if you selected a subset of the records, you can then select the option to export only those records.

If you export an object's complete record set, Access displays another dialog box, which has an option for saving the export steps. Saving the export steps saves time if you expect to run this export operation again using the same object and the same export settings.

When you export data to a text file, the steps you follow depend on whether you select the Export Data With Formatting And Layout option. When you select this option, Access displays the Encode As dialog box, which provides a choice of encoding schemes: Windows (Default), MS-DOS, Unicode, or Unicode (UTF-8). The Windows (Default) and MS-DOS options apply to text files that will be used only in programs that support these formats. Most programs consuming text files can use files encoded with the Unicode option. Unicode (UTF-8) is a format used widely on the web.

If you don't select the Export Data With Formatting And Layout option, Access displays the Export Text Wizard. In export operations that rely on the Export Text Wizard, you specify whether to export the data as a delimited text file or as a fixed-width text file.

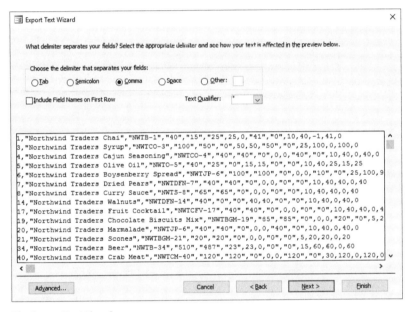

The Export Text Wizard

From this point, the Export Text Wizard displays screens that refine your initial choice. For example, for delimited text files, you specify the character that separates fields in each record (often a comma), whether to include field names in the first row of the exported file, and the text qualifier character (which is used to handle instances of the delimiting character that appear in actual values). For fixed-width exports, you use the wizard to indicate where field breaks occur by dragging lines to create columns.

When you export data to an XML file, you have the option to also export the schema for the data (an XSD file) and the presentation of the data (which is defined in an XSL file). For the data, you can export records in related tables in addition to the data in the object you selected. You can also specify an encoding scheme (UTF-8) or (UTF-16).

Among the options related to exporting the schema are whether to include table and field properties and whether to embed the schema in the XML file or create a separate schema document. Presentation options include the location where the XLS file is stored, where related images are stored, and whether the XSL transformation is run from a client or a server computer. In the Run From area, the Client option creates an HTML file on the local computer that programmatically merges the XSL file and the data (XML) file. This option does not embed the presentation information in the data, which lets you update either the XSL file or the XML file without having to run the export operation again. The Server (ASP) option creates an Active Server Pages (ASP) file that merges the presentation with the data and sends the HTML file that is created to the local computer.

You can export database objects to another Access database or in the following formats:

- For a PDF or XPS file, you can export all the object's data, selected records, or specific pages from a report. Both formats also provide options for accessibility.

- The Email option in the Export group attaches a database object to email messages in a format that you select.

- You can export the data in an object to use in a mail-merge operation in Word (the data becomes the recipient list associated with the mail merge) or save the data as a rich-text format (RTF) document.

If you expect to use an export operation regularly, you can save the export steps you defined. By saving the export steps, you can run the operation in a single step.

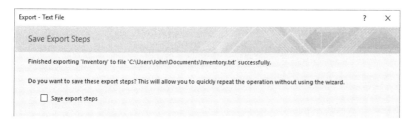

Select the Save Export Steps check box to later perform the export in a single step

When you want to run a saved export in Access, on the External Data tab, in the Export group, click Saved Exports. Access opens the Manage Data Tasks dialog box. This dialog box provides options to run the export, create an Outlook task, modify the name or description provided earlier, and delete any saved exports (or saved imports) that you no longer need.

To export data from Access

1. Open the object that contains the data you want to export.

2. On the **External Data** tab, in the **Export** group, click the format or program you want to export to.

3. In the **Export** dialog box, specify the file name and location, and select the export options you want to use: to include formatting and layout, to view the exported file, and to export only selected records.

4. Depending on the export option you select in step 2, use the options in the dialog boxes and the wizards Access provides to specify file format and related export options.

To save export steps

1. In the **Export** dialog box, select **Save export steps**.

2. Enter a name for the export steps (or accept the default name) and enter a description.

3. If you want, select **Create Outlook Task**.

4. Click **Save Export**.

To run a saved export

1. On the **External Data** tab, in the **Export** group, click **Saved Exports**.

2. In the **Manage Data Tasks** dialog box, select the export operation you want to run, and then click **Run**.

Objective 1.5 practice tasks

The practice file for these tasks is located in the **MOSAccess2016\Objective1** practice file folder. The folder also contains a result file that you can use to check your work.

➤ Open the **Access_1-5** database from the practice file folder and do the following:

- ❑ Open the Customers report from the Navigation Pane, and then display the report in print preview. Change the margins to Wide.

- ❑ Export the Customers report to Word (use the Rich Text format option).

- ❑ Export the Customers table to Excel.

- ❑ Save the **Access_1-5** database as a template. Save the template in a custom category you create named <u>MOSAccessSamples</u>.

➤ Open the **Access_1-5_results** database. Compare the two databases to check your work. Then close the open databases.

Objective group 2
Build tables

The skills tested in this section of the Microsoft Office Specialist exam for Microsoft Access 2016 relate to building tables. Specifically, the following objectives are associated with this set of skills:

- **2.1** Create tables
- **2.2** Manage tables
- **2.3** Manage records in tables
- **2.4** Create and modify fields

When you create a database, before you use Access to create tables, forms, and other database objects, it is helpful to define the tables you need, the fields that will be in each table, and how the tables are related. Considering details such as these makes the process of creating tables in Access more efficient.

You build tables by defining the table's fields and specifying data types for each field, such as Number, Currency, or Date/Time. You can also import data from external sources to create tables in your database. You work with tables in two views: Design view and Datasheet view. Design view shows only the table's structure—its fields and the data type assigned to the fields. In Datasheet view, you see the table's fields and the data the fields contain. You can adjust the view of a datasheet by hiding or freezing fields and by sorting and filtering records. To fine-tune a table, you can set field properties such as Default Value, define a validation rule that prevents users of the database from entering invalid data, or define an input mask that keeps the data entered in the field in a consistent format.

This chapter guides you in studying methods for creating tables, managing tables and records in tables, and creating and modifying fields.

> To complete the practice tasks in this chapter, you need the practice files contained in the **MOSAccess2016\Objective2** practice file folder. For more information, see "Download the practice files" in this book's introduction.

Objective 2.1: Create tables

You work with tables in two views: Design view and Datasheet view. You can create a table in either view.

In Design view, Access doesn't display data. Design view shows only the structure of a table—the fields that make up the table and the settings for properties that define the fields. Datasheet view displays data in a grid of columns and rows (resembling a worksheet in Microsoft Excel). Each column represents a field, and each row represents a record in the table.

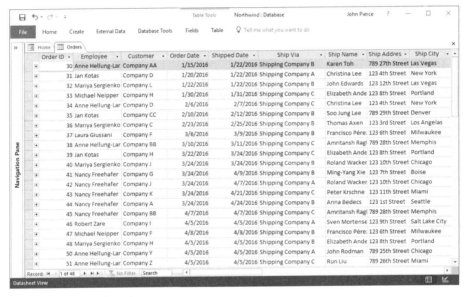

A table open in Datasheet view

This topic describes the basics of creating tables in Design view and Datasheet view. It also examines Access data types (which you apply to manage the data a field contains), provides methods for importing data to create a table, explains how to link a table to an external data source, and explains how to create a table from a template by using application parts.

Create tables

In Design view, you define the fields that a table includes by working within three main columns: Field Name, Data Type, and Description. Entering data in the first two columns is required. Adding information to the Description column is optional, but describing important fields in a table is an effective way to start documenting your database. Adding a concise explanation in the Description column also assists database users because Access displays this description in the status bar when the field is selected in Datasheet view or in a form.

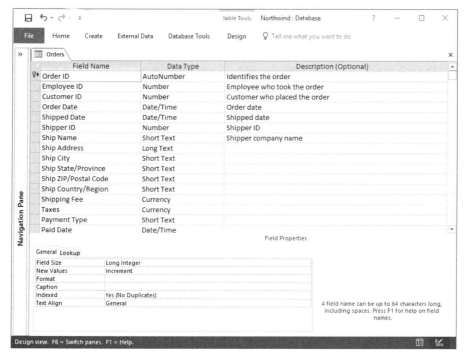

A table in Design view, with field properties defined and the OrderID field set as the table's primary key

After entering a name for a field, you assign a data type to the field. The data type you select defines and limits the kind of data you can store in the field. The following list describes Access data types:

- **Short Text** Use this data type for simple text fields, such as contact or project names or information such as street addresses or postal codes, which include numbers that aren't used in mathematical operations. By default, Access sets the Field Size property for a Short Text field to 255 characters, which is the maximum number of characters a Short Text field can contain. You can set the Field Size property to a shorter length.

- **Long Text** This data type is designed for fields in which you want to store large blocks of text. You can store approximately 1 gigabyte (GB) of alphanumeric data in a Long Text field, but not all that data will be displayed if you add this field to a form or a report—the limit is 64,000 characters.

- **Number** Use this field to store numeric data of various field sizes, including Byte, Integer, Long Integer, and Decimal. You should choose a field size according to the size and kind of numbers you will store in the field. The following field sizes are available in Access:

  - **Byte** A 1-byte integer containing values from 0 through 255.

  - **Integer** A 2-byte integer containing values from −32,768 through 32,767.

  - **Long Integer** A 4-byte integer containing values from −2,147,483,648 through 2,147,483,647.

  - **Single** A 4-byte, floating-point number containing values from −3.4 × 1,038 through 3.4 × 1,038 and up to seven significant digits.

  - **Double** An 8-byte, floating-point number containing values from −1.797 × 10,308 through 1.797 × 10,308 and up to 15 significant digits.

  - **Replication ID** A 16-byte globally unique identifier (GUID).

  - **Decimal** A 12-byte integer with a specified decimal precision that can contain values from approximately −9.999 × 1027 through 9.999 × 1027. The default precision (number of decimal places) is 0, and the default scale is 18.

- **Date/Time** This data type is designed to store dates and times. You can choose formats such as Short Date (3/08/2017) and Long Date (Monday, May 9, 2018). You can perform calculations on the data in Date/Time fields, such as determining the interval between two dates.

- **Currency** Use this data type for monetary values. You can specify formats that include up to four decimal places.

- **AutoNumber** Use this data type for fields for which you want Access to generate a unique identifying number. A table can have only one AutoNumber field, which is set to the field size Long Integer. An AutoNumber field is often used as a table's primary key.

> **See Also** For information about setting a table's primary key, see "Objective 1.2: Manage relationships and keys."

- **Yes/No** This field type is designed for fields whose value is true or false. In Yes/No fields, Access stores −1 for true (yes) or 0 for false (no).

- **OLE Object** A field with the OLE Object data type is used to store objects such as pictures or charts created in another Windows–based application. You can store objects up to about 2 GB.

- **Hyperlink** Use this data type for fields in which you want to store a website address (on the Internet or an intranet) or the path to a file on a network or the local computer.

- **Attachment** By applying this data type, you create a field in which you can store documents, spreadsheets, presentations, and other file types. You can include an unlimited number of attachments per record, although you are restricted by the limitation on the overall size of an Access database (approximately 2 GB).

- **Calculated** Use this data type for a field in which you define an expression (similar to a formula) that uses data from one or more other fields to calculate a value. Calculated fields include a Result Type property that you can use to specify the data type for the result of the calculation.

- **Lookup wizard** Use this wizard entry in the Data Type list to create a field that uses values from a related table or in a list you define. You can create a complex lookup field to store more than one value of the same data type in each record.

Tip You can set many different properties for the fields in a table. You can set some field properties when working in Datasheet view, including the Name, Caption, Description, Default Value, and Field Size properties. To work with the full range of field properties, open the table in Design view. For more information, see "Objective 2.4: Create and modify fields."

Creating a table in Design view might seem abstract. In Design view, Access displays only the definitions for the data that a table will hold but not the data itself. In contrast, by creating a table in Datasheet view, you can begin to define the structure of a table while you compile the data you want to store and manage with it. Access assigns a data type to the field based on the data you enter, or you can select a data type yourself.

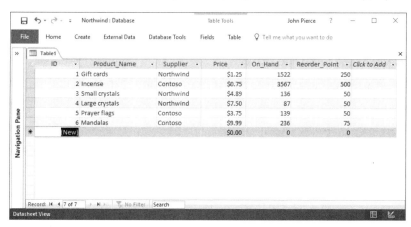

Creating a table in Datasheet view

Tip If you save a table without defining a primary key, Access displays a message box prompting you to create one so that records in the table will be uniquely identified. Click Yes to have Access add an ID field as the primary key; click No to save the table without creating a primary key.

One way to create a table is to import data. As you import data, you can define part of the structure of a table, including field names, data types, certain field properties, and the table's primary key. For example, Access can use the column headings in the source data as the table's field names.

You can import data from sources such as Excel workbooks, text files, XML files, Microsoft SharePoint lists, and Microsoft Outlook folders. When you import data, you usually have three options: importing the source data into a new table, appending the data to a table that's already defined, or linking to the data source to create a linked table.

> **See Also** For more information about importing data to create tables, see "Import database objects and data," in "Objective 1.1: Create and modify databases." For information about creating a linked table, see the next section, "Create linked tables." For information about appending data, see "Append records from external data," in "Objective 2.3: Manage records in tables."

To create a table

1. On the **Create** tab, in the **Tables** group, do either of the following:

    - To create a table that contains an ID field and open it in Design view, click **Table Design**.

    - To create a table that contains no fields and open it in Datasheet view, click **Table**.

2. Add the fields that you want to the table. If you created the table in Datasheet view, you must add at least one field.

3. On the **Quick Access Toolbar**, click **Save**.

4. In the **Save As** dialog box, enter a name for the table, and then click **OK**.

> **See Also** For information about adding fields to tables in Design view and Datasheet view, see "Objective 2.4: Create and modify fields."

Create linked tables

With linked tables, you can include in your database information that's stored in an external data source. You can create a linked table that's based on an Excel worksheet, a text file, or one of the other external data formats that Access 2016 supports. Linking to an Excel worksheet or a text file, for example, creates a one-way link. You can read the data in Access, but you cannot insert or update records—the data is maintained only in the external data source. However, you can link to tables in another Access database and work with those tables in many of the same ways you work with tables in your database. You can add and update records in a table linked to another Access database, but you can't change the table's design. To modify the design, open the table in the source database.

Access adds an entry for a linked table to the Navigation Pane, displaying an icon that identifies the type of data source. The icon includes a small arrow to indicate that the table is a linked table.

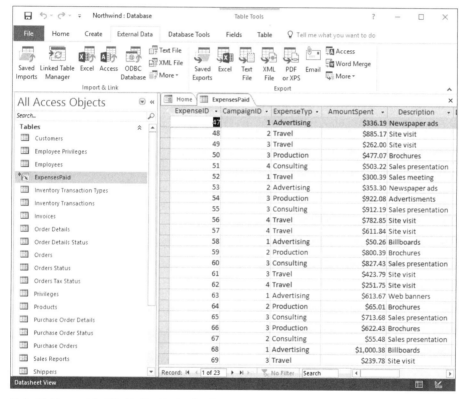

Linked tables are identified in the Navigation Pane

When you link to an Excel worksheet or a text file to create a table, Access provides a wizard (the Link Text Wizard, for example) that functions much like the wizards you follow to import data into a new table.

Tip You can link to tables in other Access databases to work around the restriction on the size of a single Access database file (approximately 2 GB).

If you link to an Access database or to another external data source that is protected with a password, you must provide the password to link successfully. Access can save the password so that you don't need to provide it each time you open the external table. Because Access saves this information, you might want to encrypt your database.

> **See Also** For more information about assigning a password to a database, see "Objective 1.4: Protect and maintain databases."

If a source file you have linked to is moved to a different location, you can update the link by using the Linked Table Manager dialog box, which lists each table linked to in the current database.

To link to a table in another Access database

1. On the **External Data** tab, in the **Import & Link** group, click **Access**.
2. In the **Get External Data** dialog box, do the following:
   a. Click **Browse** to open the File Open dialog box. Locate and select the source database, and then click **Open**.
   b. Click **Link to the data source by creating a linked table**.
   c. Click **OK** to open the Link Tables dialog box.
3. In the **Link Tables** dialog box, select the table or tables you want to link to, and then click **OK**.

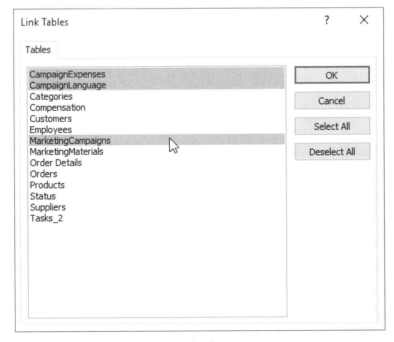

Link to one or more tables in a separate database

To link to a text file

1. On the **External Data** tab, in the **Import & Link** group, click **Text File**.

2. In the **Get External Data** dialog box, do the following:

   a. Click **Browse** to open the File Open dialog box. Locate and select the source file, and then click **Open**.

   b. Click **Link to the data source by creating a linked table**.

   c. Click **OK** to start the Link Text Wizard.

3. In the **Link Text Wizard**, do the following:

   a. On the wizard's first page, specify the format of the text file (**Delimited** or **Fixed Width**), and then click **Next**.

   b. Choose the delimiting character or specify column breaks (depending on the format).

   c. Select **First Row Contains Field Names** if this option applies.

   d. Click **Next** to work through the remaining pages to set field options.

   e. Enter a name for the linked table, and then click **Finish**.

4. In the **Link Text Wizard** message box that confirms the table was linked, click **OK**.

To link to an Excel worksheet or named range

1. On the **External Data** tab, in the **Import & Link** group, click **Excel**.

2. In the **Get External Data** dialog box, do the following:

   a. Click **Browse** to open the File Open dialog box. Locate and select the source workbook, and then click **Open**.

   b. Click **Link to the data source by creating a linked table**.

   c. Click **OK** to start the Link Spreadsheet Wizard.

3. In the **Link Spreadsheet Wizard**, do the following:

   a. On the wizard's first page, select the worksheet or named range that contains the data you want to link to, and then click **Next**.

   b. Specify whether the first column of the data includes column headings, and then click **Next**.

   c. Enter a name for the linked table, and then click **Finish**.

4. In the **Link Spreadsheet Wizard** message box that confirms the table was linked, click **OK**.

To manage linked tables

1. On the **External Data** tab, in the **Import & Link** group, click **Linked Table Manager**.

2. In the **Linked Table Manager** dialog box, select the check box for the table or tables whose links you want to update, and then click **OK**.

3. If the source file is not in the original location, Access opens the Select New Location dialog box. In the **Select New Location** dialog box, navigate to the new location for the file, select the file, and then click **Open**.

4. In the **Linked Table Manager** message box, click **OK**.

Create a table from a template by using application parts

The Quick Start group in the Application Parts gallery provides a Comments table and four compound application parts (a set of database objects) for managing contacts, issues, tasks, and users. You can apply these application parts to many types of data-bases. The ScreenTip that Access displays when you point to an item in this group identifies the objects that the application part contains. (For example, the Issues appli-cation part inserts a table named Issues and two forms.)

When you add a Quick Start application part to a database that already includes tables, Access might start the Create Relationship Wizard. (Access starts the wizard when it detects that the application part you're adding includes a table that is proba-bly related to one or more existing tables.)

> **See Also** For more information about table relationships and their purpose in an Access database, see "Objective 1.2: Manage relationships and keys."

The wizard provides two options for creating a relationship and an option that speci-fies that there is no relationship. The first option places the table you're adding on the *many* side of a one-to-many relationship. The second option places that table on the *one* side of the relationship. An often-used example of one-to-many relationships is the relationship between customers and orders. Each customer record in a database is unique (the *one* side of the relationship), but each customer record is related to all the orders placed by the customer (the *many* side of the relationship). In a one-to-many relationship, you select the two tables and the linking field. Access adds the field you specify to the table on the many side of the relationship, creating a lookup column in that table.

You can also create a group of tables and then save the tables as a database template, choosing the option to create an application part from the template. You could use this set of tables in multiple databases that store information of similar types. You can also create your own Quick Start items.

See Also For more information about database templates, see "Save a database as a template," in "Objective 1.5: Print and export data."

To create a table from a template by using application parts

1. On the **Create** tab, in the **Templates** group, click **Application Parts**.

2. In the **Application Parts** gallery, click the **Quick Start** application part you want to add.

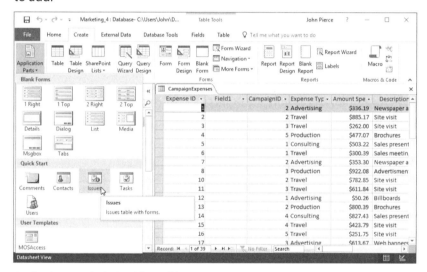

Application parts include tables and forms

3. If the Create Relationship Wizard starts, follow the steps in the wizard to either set up a relationship between the application part table and an existing table or specify that there is no relationship.

Objective 2.1 practice tasks

The practice files for these tasks are located in the **MOSAccess2016 \Objective2** practice file folder. The folder also contains a result file that you can use to check your work.

➤ Open the **Access_2-1a** database and do the following:

☐ Save the database as a template. Name the template <u>MOSAccess</u>, and select the *Application Part* option.

☐ Close the **Access_2-1a** database.

➤ Open the **Access_2-1b** database and do the following:

☐ Import the **Access_2-1c** comma-delimited text file to create a new table. Let Access create a primary key. Name the table <u>Tasks</u>.

☐ Link to the Employees table and the Compensation table from the **Access_2-1d** database.

☐ Use the *Table Design* command to create a table named <u>Status</u>.

☐ In the Status table, create an AutoNumber field named <u>StatusID</u> and use it as the table's primary key.

☐ In the Status table, create a Short Text field named <u>Status</u>.

☐ Create a table from the *MOSAccess* template application part you saved earlier.

☐ When the Create Relationship wizard prompts you to create a relationship, select There Is No Relationship, and then click Create.

➤ Open the **Access_2-1_results** database. Compare the two databases to check your work. Then close the open databases.

Objective 2.2: Manage tables

This topic covers various aspects of how you can manage a table. Managing a table involves activities such as hiding or freezing fields to make a large datasheet easier to view, and adding a Total row to display summary values for fields (a count of how many orders are recorded, for example, or the total sum or average amount of payments you've received).

Hide fields in tables

When a table includes more than 10 or so fields, you might not be able to easily view all the fields with the table open in Datasheet view. To avoid scrolling to view a field, you can hide fields you don't need to refer to (the primary key field, for example, which you would very rarely change). You can also freeze fields so that a specific field or fields remain in view as you scroll.

You can freeze a field whose column is at any position in the datasheet. Access moves the column or columns you freeze to the far left of the datasheet, placing the column or columns before any others. Unfreezing the field does not return this column (or columns) to its original position in the table. You need to drag the column heading to place the column where you want it in the table.

You can select more than one field to hide or freeze, but the fields must be adjoining fields in the datasheet. Access selects the first field you select and each field to the left or right of the next field you select.

To hide fields in a table

1. Open the table in Datasheet view.

2. Do either of the following:

   - To hide one field, right-click the field column heading, and then click **Hide Fields**.

   - To hide multiple adjacent fields, click the first field column heading, press and hold the **Shift** key, and click the last field column heading. Then right-click the selection and click **Hide Fields**.

To show hidden fields in a table

1. Open the table in Datasheet view.

2. Right-click a column heading, and then click **Unhide Fields**.

3. In the **Unhide Columns** dialog box, select the check boxes for the fields you want to show.

Unhide fields by selecting them in this dialog box

To freeze fields in a table

1. Open the table in Datasheet view.

2. Do either of the following:

   - To freeze one field, right-click the field column heading, and then click **Freeze Fields**.

   - To freeze multiple adjacent fields, click the first field column heading, press and hold the **Shift** key, and click the last field column heading. Then right-click the selection and click **Freeze Fields**.

To unfreeze fields in a table

➜ In Datasheet view, right-click a column heading, and then click **Unfreeze All Fields**.

Add Total rows

As you will learn in Objective group 3, "Create queries," one use of a query is to summarize data—that is, to count how many orders were placed in a month, for example, or to calculate the aggregate value of a number or currency field. You can also summarize data in a table by adding a Total row to display summary values for one or more fields. A Total row uses built-in functions such as Sum and Count. For Sum to be applied to a field, the field's data type must be set to Number or Currency. For fields that don't use a numeric data type (such as a text field), you can apply the Count function. In numeric fields, you can also apply the functions Average, Maximum, Minimum, Standard Deviation, and Variance.

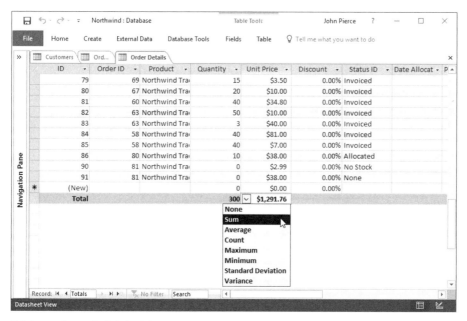

Total rows show calculated totals

To add and configure a Total row for a table

1. Open the table in Datasheet view.

2. On the **Home** tab, in the **Records** group, click **Totals**.

3. For each column in the **Total** row where you want a total to appear, click in the column, and then select the function you want to apply.

To remove the Total row from a table

→ On the **Home** tab, in the **Records** group, click **Totals**.

Add table descriptions

One of the properties you can define for a table is *Description*. Adding a description is another step you can take to document the objects and logic in your database.

You can add a description in Design view by displaying the table's property sheet or in a table's Properties dialog box.

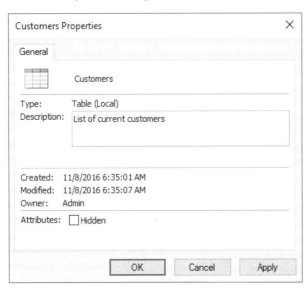

Describe a table to identify its purpose

To add a description to a table from the Navigation Pane

1. Right-click the table in the **Navigation Pane**, and then click **Table Properties**.

2. In the table's **Properties** dialog box, enter a description in the **Description** box, and then click **OK**.

To add a description to a table in Design view

1. Right-click the Design view grid, and then click **Properties**. Access displays the table's property sheet.

2. In the property sheet, click in the **Description** field, and then enter a description for the table.

Rename tables

Renaming a table requires only a couple of steps, but renaming a table (or any of the objects in your database) can produce results you don't expect. For example, the names of tables are used to define a form's record source. If a table named *Tasks* is specified as a form's record source and you rename that table, the form can't display task records unless its Record Source property is updated.

You can use the Name AutoCorrect options in the Access Options dialog box (on the Current Database page) to help manage unintended consequences caused by renaming a table. By default, Access applies two autocorrect options: Track Name AutoCorrect Info and Perform Name AutoCorrect. With these settings, Access keeps track of when an object's name changes and updates references to the object so that forms (and queries and reports) continue to retrieve the records they're designed to retrieve.

To rename a table

1. Right-click the table in the **Navigation Pane**, and then click **Rename** to activate the name for editing.

2. Enter the new table name, and then press **Enter**.

To set Name AutoCorrect options

1. Open the **Access Options** dialog box and display the **Current Database** page.

2. In the **Name AutoCorrect Options** section, do any of the following, and then click **OK**:

   - To have Access track name changes, select the **Track name AutoCorrect info** check box.

   - To have Access automatically update object names, select the **Perform name AutoCorrect** check box.

   - If you want to have Access maintain a log of the changes it makes, select **Log name AutoCorrect Changes**.

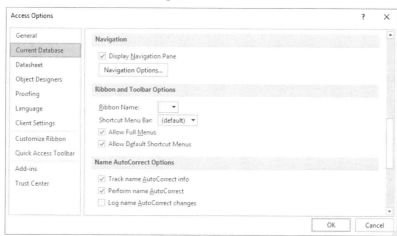

Name AutoCorrect options

Objective 2.2 practice tasks

The practice file for these tasks is located in the **MOSAccess2016\Objective2** practice file folder. The folder also contains a result file that you can use to check your work.

➤ Open the **Access_2-2** database from the practice file folder and do the following:

   ❑ If the Info bar appears, click the *Enable Content* button. In the Login Dialog window, click any name in the Select Employee list, and then click *Login*. Close the Home form, and expand the Navigation Pane.

➤ Open the Customers table in Datasheet view and do the following:

   ❑ Hide the E-mail Address, Home Phone, and Mobile Phone fields.

   ❑ Freeze the Last Name field, and then scroll to the right.

   ❑ Close the Customers table, and save your changes to the layout.

➤ Open the Orders table in Datasheet view and do the following:

   ❑ Add a Total row to the Orders table.

   ❑ In the Total row, set the Shipped Date field to display the number of orders that shipped.

➤ Close the Orders table, and then do the following:

   ❑ Add the description Our loyal customers to the Customers table.

   ❑ Turn off the *Track name AutoCorrect info* option for the database.

   ❑ Rename the Customers table as Clients, open the Customer List form, and observe the message Access displays. Then close the Customer List form.

   ❑ Rename the Clients table as Customers, and then reopen the Customer List form.

   ❑ Close the Customer List form, and then turn on the *Track name AutoCorrect Info* option for the database.

   ❑ Rename the Customers table as Clients, and then reopen the Customer List form. Then close the Customer List form.

➤ Open the **Access_2-2_results** database. Compare the two databases to check your work. Then close the open databases.

Objective 2.3: Manage records in tables

You manage the records in a table in Datasheet view. This topic describes how to add, update, and delete records and how to find, sort, and filter records when you need to work with records that match specific criteria. The topic also describes how you can append records to an existing table.

Add, update, and delete records

The actions of adding a record, updating a record's values, or deleting a record can be affected by table relationships and whether a relationship enforces referential integrity. You can't add a record to a table when a related record is required in another table—for example, you can't add the details of an order to the Order Details table unless a record for that order exists in the Orders table. Similarly, Access prevents you from deleting a record in one table (a task, for example) that creates orphan records in another table (issues related to that task).

In a relationship that enforces referential integrity, the Cascade Update Related Fields and Cascade Delete Related Records options in the Edit Relationships dialog box determine how Access manages records you update or delete. In the Northwind sample database, for example, in the relationship between the Orders and Order Details tables, Cascade Delete Related Records is selected. If you delete a record from the Orders table, related records will be deleted from the Order Details table.

See Also For information about table relationships and referential integrity, see "Objective 1.2: Manage relationships and keys."

When relationships don't restrict how you manage records (when you are first entering data in a table, for example), you work with the Records group on the Home tab to create new records, save records, and delete records. Keep in mind that you can save a record without entering data for each field, but some fields might be required. You can't save a record without entering a value in a required field.

To add a record in Datasheet view

1. On the **Home** tab, in the **Records** group, click **New**.

2. Enter the values for each field that defines the record.

3. In the **Records** group, click **Save**.

To update the value for a field

→ Select the field, and then enter the new value.

To delete a value from a specific field

→ Select the value, and then on the **Home** tab, in the **Records** group, click **Delete**.

To delete a record

→ Click the record selector (the blank cell to the left of the first field), and then on the **Home** tab, in the **Records** group, click **Delete Record**.

Append records from external data

When you import data from Excel, a text file, or an Outlook folder, you can choose an option to append records to an existing table. (You cannot append records by importing an XML file or a SharePoint list.) Access adds the records in the source data to the table you specify. The steps for importing the data are then essentially the same as when you import data into a new table.

> **See Also** For more information about importing data, see "Objective 2.1: Create tables."

To avoid errors when you append data, make sure that the external data source organization matches the structure of the table you are appending records to. For example, in an Excel worksheet that does not include column headings, the position and the type of data need to match the field order and data types in the destination table. When column headings are present, the name and data type for each column must match the corresponding fields (although the order of the columns and fields do not need to match). Also check whether the source data contains any fields not included in the table. If the source data does contain other fields, you should add these fields to the destination table or specify to skip them for the import process. The destination table can include fields that are not defined in the source data, provided those fields have their Required property set to No and the fields do not contain any validation rules that prohibit null values.

The source data must include data that is compatible with the table's primary key, and the data in that column must be unique. You receive an import error message if a primary key value in the source data matches one already defined in the destination table. Also, if the Indexed property of any field in the destination table is set to Yes (No Duplicates), the source data must include unique values for that field.

To append records to a table in the current database

1. On the **External Data** tab, in the **Import & Link** group, click one of the following data sources:

   • Excel

   • Text File

- **More**, and then **HTML Document**

- **More**, and then **Outlook Folder**

> **IMPORTANT** You can append records to a table only from Excel workbooks, text files, HTML documents, and Outlook folders.

2. In the **Get External Data** dialog box, do the following:

   a. Click **Browse** to open the File Open dialog box. Locate and select the source file, and then click **Open**.

   b. Click **Append a copy of the records to the table**, and then in the adjacent list, select the table you want to append records to.

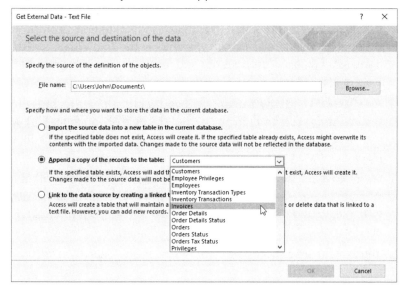

Select a table to append data

   c. Click **OK**.

3. Follow the steps in the import wizard (if Access provides one) to import and append the data.

4. In the **Get External Data** dialog box, do the following:

   a. If you want to save the steps of the operation for reuse, select the **Save import steps** check box and provide a name and optional description for the steps.

   b. Click **Close**.

Find, sort, and filter data

Over time, a database can grow to include thousands of records. Locating a specific record by scrolling through a table's datasheet (or by using a form) is inefficient in circumstances like this. To locate a record or a group of records that share specific criteria, you can use commands to find, sort, and filter records in Datasheet view.

In the Find And Replace dialog box, after you enter the value you're looking for in the Find What box, you can refine the search as follows:

- Use the Look In list to specify whether Access should search the current field or the entire table (the Current Document option).

- Use any of the following three options in the Match list:

  - **Whole Field** Use this option (the default setting) to find records with values that match the entire text string you enter in the Find What box. For example, if you enter Blue, Access does not find records whose value is Light Blue, Dark Blue, or Navy Blue.

  - **Any Part Of Field** Use this option if you want to locate records that contain the text string you enter in any part of the field. If you enter Blue with this option selected, Access finds records for Blue, Light Blue, Dark Blue, and Navy Blue (and those like them).

  - **Start Of Field** Use this option to locate records that begin with a specific string of characters—all records whose Description field starts with *Spa*, for example, to find the records for *Spanish olive oil*, *Spaghetti*, *Sparkling water*, and *Spanakopita*.

- Use the Search list to specify whether Access should search down, up, or all (both directions).

- Use the Match Case option to implement a case-sensitive search.

- Use the Search Fields As Formatted option to search a field that has a particular format or an input mask. With this option selected, Access searches the data as it is displayed instead of how Access stores it. This option is particularly useful in date and time fields.

Use the options on the Replace tab in the Find And Replace dialog box when you want to insert new data for the data Access finds. You can replace all instances of the data or a single instance.

By sorting the records in a table, you can arrange a datasheet in an order in which you can more easily find a specific record (the name of a contact) or a set of related records (all orders shipped on September 12). You can sort a field in ascending or descending order, and you can also sort a table by multiple columns. For example, you can sort a table on the Launch Date field in ascending order (January through December) and the Campaign Budget field in descending order (largest to smallest) to see the sequence of larger expenditures for campaigns scheduled to launch over a period of time. When you sort by multiple fields, apply the second, or *inner*, sort first (in this case, budgets in descending order).

Text fields provide the sorting options Sort A To Z or Sort Z To A. Number fields have the commands Sort Smallest To Largest or Sort Largest To Smallest, and date fields use Sort Oldest To Newest and Sort Newest To Oldest.

For more advanced sorts, Access displays a window with a list of the table's fields in the top pane and a grid in the bottom pane. (If you open this window when a sort order is applied, the grid shows the field and sort criteria specified.)

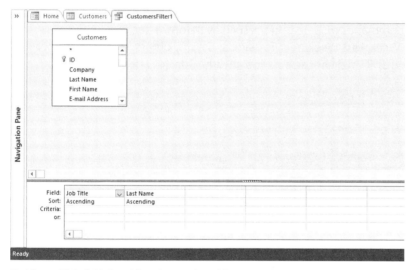

Sort by multiple fields by adding them to the grid

To sort by a field, you add it to the Field row in the grid. By adding other fields to the Field row, you can create a multiple-field sort. The Sort row provides the Ascending or Descending options, which you use to apply a sort order.

By applying a filter to a table in Datasheet view, you can select a specific set of records to review, such as all orders placed on or after a specific date or all amounts less than or greater than the target you specify.

Access provides several ways to filter records. You can filter by one or more of the values in a field, for example. Another way is to filter by selection, using either the entire value or a portion of it as the filter criterion. After selecting the criterion, you can apply an expression to apply the filter. For text fields, you can apply the expressions Equals *Value*, Does Not Equal *Value*, and Contains *Value*. For date fields, the expressions include Equals *Date*, Does Not Equal *Date*, On Or Before *Date*, On Or After *Date*, and Between, which lets you specify a date range to use as the filter. For Number fields, Less Than Or Equal To and Greater Than Or Equal To options are included along with Equals, Does Not Equal, and Between.

You can filter by selection progressively to hone in on a specific set of records. For example, the first time you apply a filter, the criteria you use might reduce 200 records to 75. Filter the remaining records by using different criteria to review a smaller subset.

Access provides additional filters based on a field's data type. The Text Filters command displays the Equals, Does Not Equal, Begins With, Does Not Begin With, Contains, Does Not Contain, Ends With, and Does Not End With filters. You choose a filter and then specify the criteria in the Custom Filter dialog box that Access displays.

The Date Filters commands include options such as Before, After, and Between, in addition to Next Week, Last Week, Year To Date, and many others. You can also choose All Dates In Period and then choose a period such as Quarter 1 or a specific month of the year.

Select a date filter to apply it to the field

Advanced filtering options include Filter By Form and Advanced Filter/Sort. When you filter by form, Access opens a blank datasheet with the names of the table's fields at the top of each column. You can then enter or select criteria for the field you want to use in the filter. You can choose a value for more than one field to create an AND condition—for example, a filter that displays records for products whose size equals Large *and* whose color equals Blue. Use the Or tab at the bottom of the window to set up additional values for the filter. If you specify filter criteria on the Or tab, Access returns records that match either the criteria specified on the Look For tab or on the Or tab.

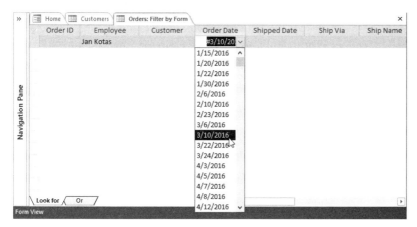

Select criteria to filter by form

In the Advanced Filter/Sort window, use the grid below the list of table fields to build filter criteria. To define the criteria, you enter an expression such as =<u>"France"</u> for a text value, or ><u>#2/14/2014#</u> for a date field.

Filters are similar to Access queries in that they define criteria that display a subset of a table's records. The similarity between filters and queries is apparent when you work with two other commands on the Advanced Filter/Sort menu: Load From Query and Save As Query. With these commands, you can use a query you've defined as a filter. Access shows the query's fields and criteria in the design grid area of the Advanced Filter/Sort window. You can also save a filter as a query that you can then run independently or include in other queries.

Tip Use the Clear Grid command on the Advanced Filter Options menu to remove any criteria from the grid.

To find records

1. Open the table in Datasheet view.

2. Do either of the following to open the Find And Replace dialog box:

   - On the **Home** tab, in the **Find** group, click **Find**.

   - Press **Ctrl+F**.

3. In the **Find and Replace** dialog box, on the **Find** tab, enter the text you want to find in the **Find What** box.

4. In the **Look In** list, select **Current field** or **Current document** (which refers to the entire table).

5. In the **Match** list, select **Whole Field**, **Any Part of Field**, or **Start of Field**.

6. In the **Search** list, select **All**, **Up**, or **Down**.

7. Select the **Match Case** check box if you want to perform a case-sensitive search.

8. Select the **Search Fields As Formatted** check box if you want to search the data as it is formatted in the datasheet.

9. Click **Find Next**.

To sort records from the Home tab

1. Open the table in Datasheet view.

2. Click the field you want to sort by.

3. On the **Home** tab, in the **Sort & Filter** group, click **Ascending** or **Descending**.

To sort records by using a shortcut menu

1. Open the table in Datasheet view.

2. Right-click the field you want to sort by, and then click the command for the sort order you want to use. (The command names depend on the field's data type.)

To set up and apply an advanced sort

1. Open the table in Datasheet view.

2. On the **Home** tab, in the **Sort & Filter** group, click **Advanced**, and then click **Advanced Filter/Sort**.

3. In the **Advanced Filter/Sort** window, drag the field or fields you want to sort by to the **Field** row in the grid.

4. In the **Sort** row, select the sort order you want to use.

5. In the **Sort & Filter** group, click **Toggle Filter** to sort the records.

6. Click **Remove Sort** to return the table to its default sort order.

To filter by a field in Datasheet view

1. Do either of the following to display the Sort & Filter menu for the field you want to filter by:

   - Select the field you want to filter by, and then on the **Home** tab, in the **Sort & Filter** group, click **Filter**.

   - In the field header of the field you want to filter by, click the arrow.

2. On the **Sort & Filter** menu, clear the **(Select All)** check box.

3. Select the check box for each field value you want to view, and then click **OK** to apply the filter.

To filter by selection in Datasheet view

1. Select the value or the portion of a value you want to use as the filter.

2. On the **Home** tab, in the **Sort & Filter** group, click the **Selection** button, and then click **Equals** "*value*", **Does Not Equal** "*value*", **Contains** "*value*", or "**Does Not Contain** "*value*". (Clicking **Toggle Filter** removes the filter from the table.)

To filter by form

1. On the **Home** tab, in the **Sort & Filter** group, click **Advanced**, and then click **Filter By Form**.

2. In the **Filter by Form** window, on the **Look for** tab, enter the value in the field or fields you want to use as the filter.

3. Click the **Or** tab to set up alternative conditions.

4. In the **Sort & Filter** group, click **Toggle Filter** to apply the filter. (Clicking **Toggle Filter** again removes the filter.)

To create an advanced filter

1. On the **Home** tab, in the **Sort & Filter** group, click **Advanced**, and then click **Advanced Filter/Sort**.

2. In the **Advanced Filter/Sort** window, in the **Field** row in the grid, select the fields you want to use in the filter.

3. In the **Criteria** row, specify the expression to use in the filter.

4. In the **Sort & Filter** group, click **Toggle Filter** to apply the filter. (Clicking **Toggle Filter** again removes the filter.)

To use a query as a filter

1. On the **Home** tab, in the **Sort & Filter** group, click **Advanced**, and then click **Advanced Filter/Sort**.

2. Click **Advanced** again, and then choose **Load from Query**.

3. In the **Applicable Filter** dialog box, select the query you want to use as a filter, and then click **OK**.

4. In the **Sort & Filter** group, click **Toggle Filter** to apply the filter. (Clicking **Toggle Filter** again removes the filter.)

To save a filter as a query

1. On the **Home** tab, in the **Sort & Filter** group, click **Advanced**, and then click **Advanced Filter/Sort**.

2. In the **Advanced Filter/Sort** window, in the **Field** row in the grid, select the fields you want to use in the filter.

3. In the **Criteria** row, specify the expression to use in the filter.

4. Click **Advanced**, and then choose **Save As Query**.

5. Enter a name for the query in the **Save As Query** dialog box, and then click **OK**.

Objective 2.3 practice tasks

The practice files for these tasks are located in the **MOSAccess2016 \Objective2** practice file folder. The folder also contains a result file that you can use to check your work.

➤ Open the **Access_2-3a** database from the practice file folder and do the following:

- ❑ Open the CampaignExpenses table in Datasheet view.

- ❑ Add a new record for Campaign ID 3, with the Expense Type set to *Consulting* and the amount $509.96. Enter the description <u>Sales presentation</u>, and today's date. Select the ApprovalRequired field to note that the expenditure requires approval.

- ❑ Sort the table records in ascending order by the Description field.

- ❑ Filter the table to show only records that have an ExpenseType of *Travel*.

- ❑ Create an advanced filter by using criteria that filters for expense types equal to *Travel* and the amount spent greater than $800 (*>800*). Apply the filter, and then save the filter as a query with the name <u>MajorTravelExpenses</u>.

- ❑ Append the data in the **Access_2-3b** spreadsheet to the CampaignExpenses table.

➤ Open the **Access_2-3_results** database. Compare the two databases to check your work. Then close the open databases.

Objective 2.4: Create and modify fields

Table fields are defined not only by their name and data type. *Field properties* add to the definition of a field by specifying a format (as for Date/Time fields), whether a field is required, whether Access creates an index for that field, the field's default value, and other information.

This topic expands on how tables are defined. It describes how you create and delete fields and how you work with field properties to fine-tune a table's design. You study how to set field sizes and captions, input masks, field validation rules, and default values. This section also describes how to increment the value in a field automatically and how to change a field's data type.

You can accomplish most of the tasks described in this section with the table open in Design view or in Datasheet view.

Add and delete fields

In Design view, you can add a field by entering the field name in the first blank row or insert a row where you want the field to appear. (A row is inserted above the row you select.) If you delete a field that contains data, Access prompts you to confirm this action, warning that you will permanently delete the field and its data.

When a table is open in Datasheet view, you add and delete fields in a couple of ways. The Click To Add column heading displays a list of field data types you can apply to the field. You can also add fields by working with commands in the Add & Delete group on the Table Tools Fields tool tab. A field you insert appears to the right of the field selected in the table. The Add & Delete group provides options that correspond to Access data types. Use the Short Text, Number, Currency, Date/Time, and Yes/No options to insert a field and apply that data type. (The Number command inserts a field whose Field Size property is set to Long Integer.) The More Fields command opens a menu that provides additional data types, including Attachment, Hyperlink, and Long Text, plus a variety of formats for the Number, Date/Time, and Yes/No data types.

The last category in the More Fields list is the Quick Start group. Similar to the Quick Start application parts described earlier in this chapter, these Quick Start items contain one or more fields that are assigned appropriate data types. You can add Quick Start items (also known as *data type application parts*) to a table to define a group of related fields.

In fields provided by Quick Start data types, many field properties are set so that you can start using the fields to capture data without additional work. For example, the Address item adds fields named Address, City, State Province, ZIP Postal, and Country Region. (You can rename the fields to fit your database.) The Payment Type item inserts a lookup field that includes the list Cash, Credit Card, Check, and In-Kind.

You can also create your own Quick Start data types. Data type application parts that you create are stored in the default location for Access database templates (usually AppData\Roaming\Microsoft\Templates under your user profile) and use the .accft file name extension. You can share these files so that colleagues and coworkers can also work with the data types you create.

See Also For information about renaming database objects, see "Rename tables" in "Objective 2.2: Manage tables."

The Add & Delete group also includes a Delete button. Keep in mind that Access prevents you from deleting a field that is part of a relationship and displays a message box informing you that you must delete the relationship first.

To add fields to tables in Design view

1. In the **Field Name** column, enter the name of the field, and then press **Tab**.
2. In the **Data Type** column, select the data type for the field, and then press **Tab**.
3. In the **Description** column, enter a brief description of the field, and then press **Tab**.
4. In the **Field Properties** area, set properties such as Field Size, Format, Indexed, and Required.

To insert a field in an existing table in Design view

→ Right-click the existing field that is in the location where you want to insert the new field, and then click **Insert Row**.

To add fields to tables in Datasheet view

1. Click the **Click to Add** arrow, and then select the data type you want to apply to the field.
2. Replace the **Field**N column heading with the name of the field.
3. Repeat steps 1 and 2 to add additional fields to the table.

Or

1. Select the field that you want to insert the new field after.
2. On the **Fields** tool tab, in the **Add & Delete** group, click the data type for the field you want to insert. Click **More Fields** to display an extended list of data types.
3. In the column heading row, replace the placeholder name (FieldN) with the name of the field.
4. Save and name the table.

To insert a Quick Start data type in Datasheet view

1. Select the field that you want to insert the new fields after.

2. On the **Fields** tool tab, in the **Add & Delete** group, click **More Fields**, and in the **Quick Start** section of the menu, click the field or field set you want to insert.

To define a custom data type application part

1. In the datasheet, select the field or fields you want to include in the custom data type.

2. On the **Fields** tool tab, in the **Add & Delete** group, click **More Fields**, and then click **Save Selection as New Data Type**.

3. In the **Create New Data Type from Fields** dialog box, enter a name and description for the custom data type. Select an entry in the **Category** list, or enter the name for a new category. Then click **OK**.

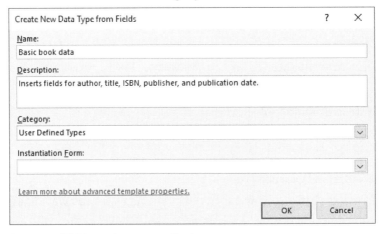

Save a set of fields as a data type application part

To rename a field in Datasheet view

1. Right-click the field heading, and then click **Rename Field** to activate the field name for editing.

2. Enter the new field name, and then press **Enter**.

To delete a field in Datasheet view

1. Right-click the field heading, and then click **Delete Field**.

2. When Access prompts you to confirm that you want to delete the field, click **Yes**.

To rename a field in Design view

→ In the **Field Name** column, select the field name, and then enter the new name.

To delete a field in Design view

1. Right-click the row selector to the left of the field name, and then click **Delete Row**.

2. When Access prompts you to confirm that you want to delete the field, click **Yes**.

Add validation rules to fields

The data type you assign to a field prevents some erroneous data entry. For example, enter the text "test" in a Date/Time field, and Access displays a warning telling you that the value does not match the Date/Time data type. You can define a validation rule for a field to further control the data a user can enter. Validation rules don't apply for all types of fields. You use them most often for fields that use the Short Text, Number, Currency, or Date/Time data types.

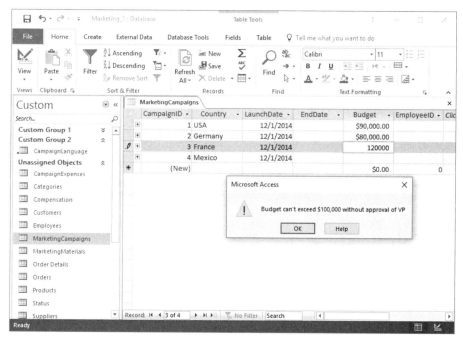

Using a validation rule and message

A simple validation rule might compare the value of a field to one or more constants. For example, enter the expression <1000 as a field validation rule to ensure that the field contains no values greater than 1,000. Be sure to enclose text strings in quotation marks, and enclose dates with pound signs (#). For example, you can create a validation rule that specifies a list of valid values for a product size field by using the expression *"Large" OR "Medium" OR "Small"*. For a Date/Time field, the expression *BETWEEN #1/1/2017# and #12/31/2017#* sets the field validation rule so that only dates in calendar year 2017 are valid.

You can use the LIKE operator and wildcard characters to specify a valid pattern. For example, for a five-digit US ZIP Code, use the expression *LIKE "#####"*. You can also define an error message that Access displays when invalid data is entered in the field.

To add a field validation rule in Datasheet view

1. Open the table in Datasheet view and select the field you want to add the rule to.

2. On the **Fields** tool tab, in the **Field Validation** group, click the **Validation** arrow, and then click **Field Validation Rule**.

3. In the Expression Builder, enter the expression that defines the rule, and then click **OK**.

To create a validation message

1. On the **Fields** tool tab, in the **Field Validation** group, click the **Validation** arrow, and then click **Field Validation Message**.

2. In the **Enter Validation Message** dialog box, enter the message that Access displays if users enter invalid data, and then click **OK**.

To add a field validation rule in Design view

1. Open the table in Design view and select the field you want to add the rule to.

2. In the **Field Properties** area, in the **Validation Rule** property box, enter the expression for the validation rule.

3. In the **Validation Text** property box, enter the message you want Access to display if users enter invalid data.

Modify field properties

By default, a field's name identifies the field in the column heading in Datasheet view or when the field is added to a form or a report. You can enter a caption to change the display name for the field. For example, a database designer might name fields by using internal capitalization, such as *TaskName*. To make the field's name more readable on forms and reports, enter <u>Task Name</u> as the field's caption.

The Field Size property for a field that uses the Short Text data type specifies the maximum number of characters that can be entered in the field. For example, suppose your company uses a six-character product code, with a combination of letters and numbers. You could set the Field Size property to 6 to ensure that no user enters more characters than are allowed.

For a Number field, the Field Size property specifies the extent of the numbers the field can contain (for example, Byte, Long Integer, and Single).

By using the Default Value command in Datasheet view (or the Default Value property box in Design view), you define the value that Access enters automatically for a field. For example, you might use the built-in function *Now()* in an order date field to fill in today's date when a new order is entered. You can also use a text or numerical constant as a field's default value. For example, you could set a default value for a country/region field so that the field is set automatically to the value you use most often. Likewise, if you sold certain products only with a minimum order quantity (only in units of 12, for example), you could set the Default Value property in the quantity field to reflect that amount.

In building a table, the best approach is to set the data type for a field once and not change it. Changing a field's data type can be problematic, especially after data has been added to a table. For example, if you change the data type for a Date/Time field to a Number field, the dates are converted to their serial value (12/31/2016 becomes 42735). Access can handle the conversion of dates to numbers (and back to dates), but other data types don't work as smoothly. Access displays a warning if you change a field's data type from Long Text to Short Text, telling you that some data will be lost.

To change a field caption

→ In Datasheet view, on the **Fields** tool tab, in the **Properties** group, click **Name & Caption**.

→ In Design view, enter the caption in the **Caption** property box.

To change a field size

→ In Datasheet view, to change the field size for a text field, click the **Fields** tool tab and then select the field. In the **Properties** group, enter the field size in the **Field Size** box.

→ In Design view, select the field, and then, in the **Field Properties** area, click in the **Field Size** property box. For a number field, select the field size setting from the list Access provides; for a text field, enter the value you want to use.

To set the default value for a field

→ In Datasheet view, on the **Fields** tool tab, in the **Properties** group, click **Default Value** to open the Expression Builder, and then enter the default value or use the Expression Builder to create an expression that calculates the default value.

→ In Design view, in the **Field Properties** area, click in the **Default Value** property box, and then do either of the following:

  • Enter the default value.

  • Click the ellipsis button (...) in the property box to open the Expression Builder, and then enter the value or expression there.

To change the data type of a field

→ In Design view, select the new value in the **Data Type** list.

→ In Datasheet view, on the **Fields** tool tab, in the **Formatting** group, expand the **Data Type** list, and then click the data type you want.

Automate field values and formatting

Assign the AutoNumber data type to a field to have Access add a unique number in that field as you add records to a table. AutoNumber is often assigned to an ID field that is used as the table's primary key.

A table can include only one AutoNumber field whose Field Size property is set to Long Integer. (You can use the AutoNumber data type for other fields if the Field Size property is set to Replication ID.) In Design view, check the setting for the New Values property for an AutoNumber field. The default setting is Increment, which means Access assigns numbers sequentially. The Random setting produces random numbers for new records. You might use the Random setting to create unique order IDs.

An input mask defines a specific pattern for the data in a field. Adding an input mask to a field assists users with entering data correctly. Access provides input masks for data such as phone numbers, US Social Security numbers, ZIP Codes, passwords, and date formats. It is important to remember that an input mask does not affect how data is stored. A field's data type and other properties define that format. An input mask affects only whether the data has been entered in a format Access will accept.

The Input Mask Wizard lists the input masks available for the data type of the currently selected field. For a Date/Time field, Access provides entries such as Long Time, Short Date, and Medium Date. For Short Text fields, the list includes input masks for phone numbers, ZIP Codes, and other sorts of data.

Input Mask Wizard

Which input mask matches how you want data to look?

To see how a selected mask works, use the Try It box.

To change the Input Mask list, click the Edit List button.

Input Mask:	Data Look:
Long Time	1:12:00 PM
Short Date	9/27/1969
Short Time	13:12
Medium Time	01:12 PM
Medium Date	27-Sep-69

Try It: |__-__-__

| Edit List | Cancel | < Back | Next > | Finish |

Input masks keep data consistent

You can enter sample data in the Try It box to view how the mask controls data entry. For example, select the Short Date mask, and then enter a month abbreviation in the Try It box. You can specify how an input mask is designed by using special characters to define the mask. In a mask, a zero (0) indicates that a user must enter a digit (from 0 through 9) in that placeholder. A nine (9) marks an optional digit. An uppercase L is used to denote a required letter. An optional letter is marked with a question mark (?). You can create an input mask of your own by using the defined special characters to set up the mask.

See Also You can find a complete list of special characters and how to use them in the article "Guide data entry in Access by using input masks" on the Office support site at *https://support.office.com*.

To configure a field to automatically increment the field value

1. Open the table in Design view, and select the field you want to automatically increment.

2. Set the field data type to **AutoNumber**.

3. In the **Field Properties** area, expand the **New Values** property list, and then click **Increment**.

To specify an input mask for a field

1. Open the table in Design view, and select the field you want to apply an input mask to.

2. Click in the **Input Mask** property box, and then click the ellipsis to start the Input Mask Wizard.

3. Work through the wizard to select the mask you want to use, or click **Edit List** to modify a built-in mask or create one of your own.

Objective 2.4 practice tasks

The practice file for these tasks is located in the **MOSAccess2016 \Objective2** practice file folder. The folder also contains a result file that you can use to check your work.

➤ Open the **Access_2-4** database and do the following:

☐ Open the Customers table in Datasheet view.

☐ Select the fields Company Name, Contact Name, and Contact Title, and then create a Quick Start data type named <u>Contact Basics</u>.

☐ Create a new table in Design view. Add a field named *ContactID*. Set the field to the *AutoNumber* data type and mark this field as the table's primary key. Save the table, and name it <u>Contacts</u>.

☐ Switch to Datasheet view, and then add the *Contact Basics* data type application part to the Contacts table. Save and close the table.

☐ Open the CampaignExpenses table in Design view. Create a validation rule for the AmountSpent field so that amounts entered must be less than $1,200. Enter the validation text <u>The amount is too large!</u>

☐ Save the table, and then switch to Datasheet view.

☐ Update the Amount Spent field in the first record to $1,200.01, and then click away from the field. Observe the message Access displays. Click *OK* in the message box, and then update the value to $1,199.99.

☐ For the CampaignExpenses table, use the *Name & Caption* command to update the *Caption* property for the DatePurchased field so that it reads <u>Purchase Date</u>.

☐ Save the table, and then switch to Design view.

☐ Change the format of the DatePurchased field to *Medium Date*.

☐ Create an input mask for the DatePurchased field that uses the Medium Date format.

➤ Open the **Access_2-4_results** database. Compare the two databases to check your work. Then close the open databases.

Objective group 3
Create queries

The skills tested in this section of the Microsoft Office Specialist exam for Microsoft Access 2016 relate to creating and using queries. Specifically, the following objectives are associated with this set of skills:

3.1 Create queries

3.2 Modify queries

3.3 Create calculated fields and grouping within queries

Queries help you analyze data, locate records that match specific criteria, and manage database records. For example, you can run a query to delete records or to append data to a table. With a select query, you can view a specific set of records (for example, only orders placed within the past 90 days that exceed a certain dollar amount). Queries also provide ways with which you can calculate totals and group and summarize data.

This chapter guides you in studying ways to create and modify queries, create calculated fields, and group within queries.

3

To complete the practice tasks in this chapter, you need the practice files contained in the **MOSAccess2016\Objective3** practice file folder. For more information, see "Download the practice files" in this book's introduction.

Objective 3.1: Create queries

You can create a query in Design view or use a wizard to create most or all of the query for you. (Access provides wizards that you use to create different kinds of queries.) In the Query Designer, you add the tables and fields a query requires and define criteria that Access applies to display or act on a specific set of records.

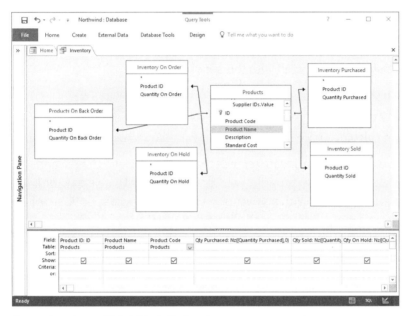

A query based on multiple tables in Design view

This topic describes how to run a query and how to save and delete a query. You also examine how to create various types of queries, including select queries, crosstab queries, parameter queries, action queries, and queries that use multiple tables.

Run queries

You can run a query directly from the Navigation Pane or by using commands. Running a query displays the query results in Datasheet view, where you can then sort and filter the records, export the query's data, and perform other operations.

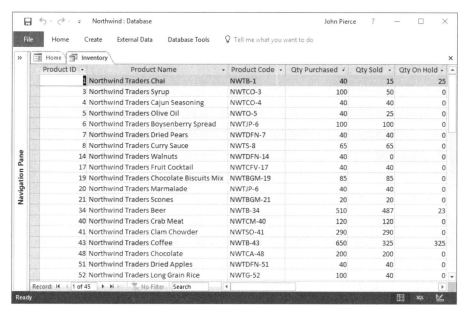

Run a query to see its results in Datasheet view

When you work in the Query Designer, as you add or remove fields and define criteria and other query properties, you can run the query to view the records that the query returns. You can then return to Design view to make additional modifications to the query and run the query again to check the effects of the changes.

To run a query from the Navigation Pane

→ Double-click the query.

→ Right-click the query, and then click **Open**.

To run a query from Design view

1. Open the query in Design view.

2. On the **Design** tool tab, in the **Results** group, click **Run**.

Create select queries

A select query is often the basis for other types of queries, including crosstab queries and action queries. A *select query* returns all or a subset of the records stored in one or more tables. When you create a select query, you specify which fields you want to use, and you can define criteria to return a specific set of records. One simple illustration of a select query is as a record source for a mailing list. For example, by using a contacts table as the basis for the query, you could include name, address, and related fields in the query without adding fields for a contact's email address and phone number. If you're sending a mailing to contacts in specific locations, you could define criteria that limits the records the query returns to contacts in the locations or postal codes you designate.

Exam Strategy   Select queries are the basis of other types of queries described in this chapter, including crosstab queries and action queries. In Exam 77-730, "Access 2016: Core Database Management, Manipulation, and Query Skills," you might not need to specifically demonstrate how to create a select query, but you will need the skills described in this section to create other types of queries.

See Also   For more information about using criteria to filter the records in a query, see "Set filter criteria" in "Objective 3.3: Create calculated fields and grouping within queries."

Select queries (and other types of queries) also illustrate one purpose of table rela-tionships. You can add two or more tables to a query and use their relationship to retrieve a set of records from all the tables—for example, all high-priority tasks related to projects for a particular customer, managed by a specific employee, and with a completion date within 30 days.

See Also   For more information about queries that use multiple tables, see "Create multiple-table queries" later in this topic.

To create a select query, you can use the Simple Query Wizard or create the query in the Query Designer. In the Query Designer, you can add criteria to the query. The wizard provides an option that opens the Query Designer if you need it.

The Simple Query Wizard tailors its steps based on factors such as the following:

- If you add fields from only one table and those fields store only text data (not numeric data), the wizard prompts you to name the query and specify whether to open the query to view the records it returns or open the query in Design view for modification.

- If you include numeric or date fields or fields from more than one table, the wizard prompts you to create a detail query or a summary query. A detail query shows each individual record that the query returns. In a summary query, you can total the values in a field or determine the field's average, minimum, or maximum value.

- When date fields are present in a summary query, the wizard also prompts you to choose an option for how you want to group records by dates. For example, you can group records by month, quarter, or year.

See Also For more information about summary queries and grouping records in a query, see "Objective 3.3: Create calculated fields and grouping within queries."

When you open the Query Designer, it displays the query design grid and the Show Table dialog box. The Show Table dialog box lists all the tables and queries in the current database.

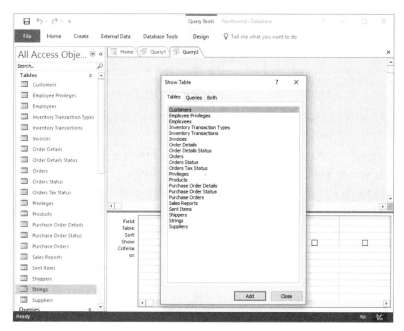

Queries are based on tables or other queries

When you add more than a few tables to a query, you can reposition the field lists in the main pane of the Query Designer to view more clearly the relationship lines that link the tables. You add a field to the query by dragging it from the field list in the main pane to the Field row in a blank column in the grid at the bottom of the Query Designer, or you can select fields from the list displayed in the Field row. The asterisk at the top of the field list adds all the fields in a table to the query design grid.

By default, a query returns all matching records, but you can select a preset value (5, 25, 100, 5%, or 25%) or enter a value to specify how many records you want to display. By limiting the number of records, you can view data such as the top 20 orders that customers placed in the current month.

To create a select query by using the Simple Query Wizard

1. On the **Create** tab, in the **Queries** group, click **Query Wizard**.

2. In the **New Query** dialog box, with **Simple Query Wizard** selected in the list of wizards, click **OK**.

3. In the **Simple Query Wizard**, expand the **Tables/Queries** list and select the first table or query you want to use for this query.

4. In the **Available Fields** list, do either of the following:

   - Select the field or fields you want to include in the query, and then click the arrow button (>) to move the fields to the **Selected Fields** list.

   - Click the chevron button (>>) to move all the fields to the **Selected Fields** list.

5. Repeat steps 3 and 4 to include other tables or queries in the select query and add the fields you want to include. Then click **Next**.

6. If the query includes numeric fields or fields from more than one table, the wizard prompts you to create a detail query or a summary query. A detail query is the default option. To continue creating a detail query, click **Next**. To create a summary query, do the following:

   a. Select the **Summary** option, and then click **Summary Options** to display a list of the affected fields.

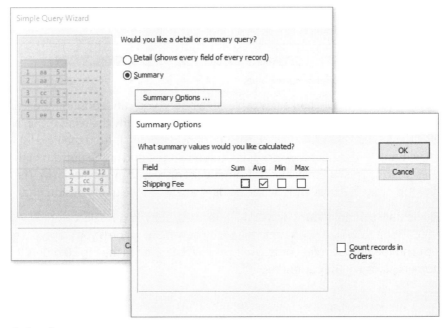

Options for a summary query

   b. In the **Summary Options** dialog box, select the check box for each summary function you want to apply to each of the fields.

   c. Click **OK** to close the Summary Options dialog box and return to the wizard.

7. Click **Next** in the wizard.

8. If the query includes a Date/Time field, click an option to specify the way you want to group dates in the query, and then click **Next**.

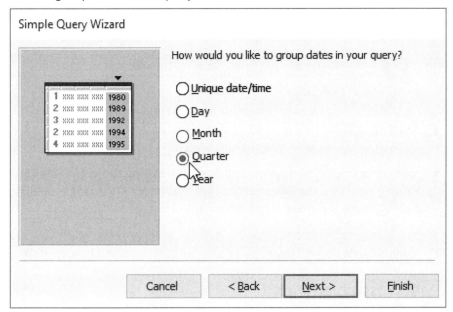

Options for grouping records by date

9. On the wizard's last page, enter a name for the query, choose whether to open the query to review the results or open the query in Design view, and then click **Finish**.

To create a select query in Design view

1. On the **Create** tab, in the **Queries** group, click **Query Design**.

2. In the **Show Table** dialog box, select the tables or queries you want to use in the query. Click **Add** to add the objects to the **Query Designer**, and then click **Close**.

3. To add fields to the query, do one of the following:

- From the field lists in the main pane, drag the fields you want to include in the query to the **Field** row in the query design grid. Access adds the field and table or query name to the grid.

    Tip You can display or hide the table row by clicking the Table Names button in the Show/Hide group on the Design tool tab.

- Click in the **Field** row of the query design grid, click the arrow, and then select the field from the list.

    Tip Each field is preceded by the table or query name.

- To add all fields in a field list to the query, double-click or drag the asterisk from the field list in the main pane to the **Field** row.

4. In the **Criteria** row and the **Or** row, define selection criteria for the query depending on which records you want the query to return.

5. To return a specific number of records, on the **Design** tool tab, in the **Query Setup** group, click the **Return** arrow, and then select the option you want to apply, or enter the value in the **Return** box.

6. On the **Quick Access Toolbar**, click **Save**.

7. In the **Save As** dialog box, enter a name for the query, and then click **OK**.

Create crosstab queries

A crosstab query uses Sum, Avg, or another aggregate function to group a query's results. In Datasheet view, a crosstab query looks something like a PivotTable in Microsoft Excel. The query's data is grouped by two sets of values, based on fields you select. One set appears down the left side of the datasheet, and the other appears across the top. The values in the body of the query come from the field you designate as the Value field.

See Also For more information about using Sum, Avg, or other aggregate functions in a query, see "Group and summarize query records" in "Objective 3.3: Create calculated fields and grouping within queries."

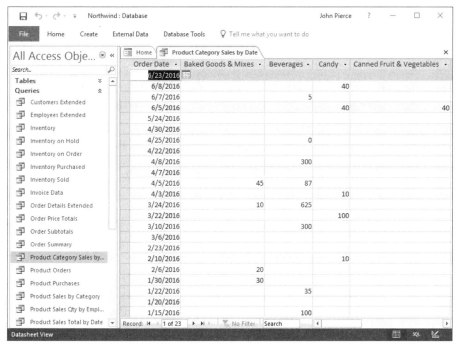

A crosstab query summarizing quantities by date and category

Access provides a wizard you can use to create a crosstab query, or you can use the Query Designer to specify the fields for the query and to define the calculations you want the query to perform. When you add fields to a crosstab query, you specify which fields to use as row headings (you can use as many as three fields), which field appears in the columns across the top, and which field is used for the summary values.

You can select fields from only one table or query when you use the Crosstab Query Wizard. To work around this limitation, you can create a select query that includes fields from multiple tables and then choose the select query as the record source when you work in the Crosstab Query Wizard.

In the wizard, you must identify the following information:

- The table or query on which to base the crosstab query.

- The field or fields (up to three fields) you want to use as row headings. If you use more than one field, Access sorts the query's records in the order in which you select the fields. Keep in mind that using more than one field makes the query more difficult to read.

- The field you want to use for the column headings. It's generally good practice to choose a field that includes only a few values for the column heading field. For example, you might select a task status field with values such as Not Started, In Progress, and Complete.

- The interval for grouping date/time information in the column headings (if you choose a Date/Time field for the column heading). You can choose Year, Quarter, Month, Date, or Date/Time.

- The field whose value you want to summarize and the function you want to apply. Different functions are available depending on the field's data type. This page of the wizard also includes the option Yes, Include Row Sums. Selecting this check box inserts a row heading in the query that uses the same field and function as the field value. A row sum also inserts a column that summarizes the remaining columns.

- The name you want to assign to the query.

When you create a crosstab query in Design view, you can include multiple tables or queries as the query's record source. You can also first create a select query that returns the records you want and use that query as the sole record source for the crosstab query.

> **See Also** For information about creating select queries, see "Create select queries" earlier in this topic.

The design grid for a crosstab query contains a Total row and a Crosstab row (in addition to the Sort, Criteria, and Or rows you work with in select queries). You use the Crosstab row to specify which field or fields to use as row headings, which field to use for the query's column headings, and which field to summarize for the query's values. In the Total row, you specify the summary function that the query applies.

To create a crosstab query by using the Crosstab Query Wizard

1. On the **Create** tab, in the **Queries** group, click **Query Wizard**.

2. In the **New Query** dialog box, select **Crosstab Query Wizard**, and then click **OK**.

3. On the wizard's first page, select the table or query on which to base the cross-tab query, and then click **Next**.

4. Specify the field or fields (up to three fields) you want to use as row headings, and then click **Next**.

5. Select the field you want to use for the column headings, and then click **Next**.

6. If you chose a Date/Time field for the column heading in step 5, specify the interval for grouping date/time information in the column headings, and then click **Next**.

7. Select the field whose value you want to summarize and the function you want to apply, and then click **Next**.

8. Enter a name for the query, and then click **Finish**.

To create a crosstab query in Design view

1. On the **Create** tab, in the **Queries** group, click **Query Design**.

2. In the **Show Table** dialog box, select the tables or queries you want to use in the query. Click **Add** to add the tables to the **Query Designer**, and then click **Close**.

3. From the table field lists, drag the fields you want to include in the query to the **Field** row in the query design grid. (You can also select fields from the list Access displays when you click in the **Field** row in the query design grid.)

4. In the **Criteria** row, define any selection criteria for the query.

5. On the **Design** tool tab, in the **Query Type** group, click **Crosstab**.

6. In the **Crosstab** row, specify the field or fields you want to use for row headings, column headings, and the query's values.

7. In the **Total** row for the value field, select the summary function you want to apply.

8. On the **Design** tool tab, in the **Results** group, click **Run** to display the query's results.

Create parameter queries

A parameter query provides flexibility in applying criteria. Instead of adding criteria such as *="Los Angeles"* to the City field, you define a parameter for that field by using a format and a prompt such as *[Enter City Name]*. When you run a parameter query, Access opens the Enter Parameter Value dialog box, which displays the prompt you defined. You can enter the value you want to use as criteria (for example, *Minneapolis* or *Montreal* for the city parameter). Access returns the set of records that match the criteria you provide.

3

When you create a parameter query, you also specify the parameter's data type, which should match the data type for the field you defined the parameter for.

Tip You can also use parameters in crosstab, append, make-table, and update queries.

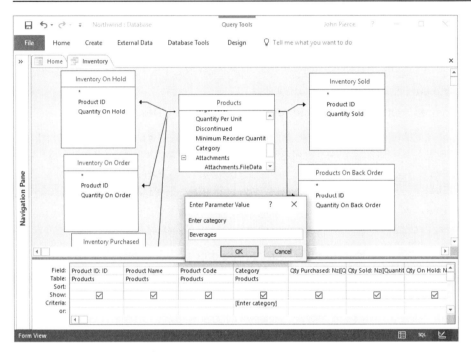

Use a parameter query to specify criteria when you run the query

To create a parameter query

1. On the **Create** tab, in the **Queries** group, click **Query Design**.

2. In the **Show Table** dialog box, add the tables you want to use in the query.

3. Add the fields you need to the query.

4. In the **Criteria** row for the field you want to use as a parameter, enter the parameter prompt, enclosing the prompt in square brackets.

5. On the **Design** tool tab, in the **Show/Hide** group, click **Parameters**.

6. In the **Query Parameters** dialog box, in the **Parameter** column, enter the parameter prompt exactly as it appears in the design grid. In the **Data Type** column, select the data type for the parameter, and then click **OK**.

Create action queries

Action queries are often used to help manage the records in a database. For example, you can use a select query to retrieve records for all discontinued products. You can use a make-table or an append query—two types of action queries—to archive those records. You can run an update or a delete query to update the value of a field or to remove records that match criteria you define.

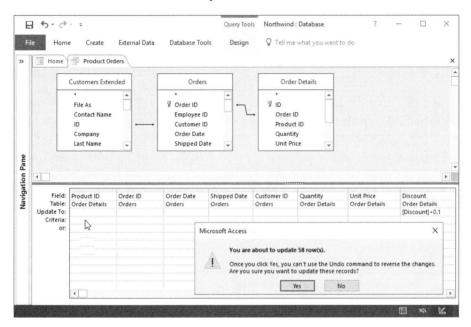

Access displays a warning before you run an action query

When you run a make-table query, Access creates a table (in the current database or in another database you designate) that's defined by the fields included in the query. A make-table query has at least a couple of functions:

- A make-table query can improve the performance of your database when you find yourself frequently running a select query that is based on several tables whose data doesn't change. Access can run the select query more quickly if it is based on a single table (created by the make-table query) instead of on multiple tables.

- You can use a make-table query to build your data archives. For example, use a make-table query to store all the orders for the past year and use the Orders table only for current orders.

A table created by a make-table query inherits field names and data types but not all settings specified for other field properties. Also, the new table does not include a primary key. Open the new table in Design view to update field properties and assign a primary key.

See Also For information about how to set a primary key, see "Objective 1.2: Manage relationships and keys."

Because a make-table query is based on a select query, you can run the select query first to review the records the query returns and then run the make-table query. You can run a make-table query more than once. When you do, the existing table is deleted.

An append query is similar to a make-table query, but instead of creating a table, an append query adds records to a table that is already defined. Append queries are also useful tools for archiving records. For example, you could create a table named Completed Projects and then design a query based on the Projects table and related tables to select the records you want. By running this query periodically as an append query, you create an archive of completed projects.

You can append records to a table in the current database or a different database you specify. When you create an append query, keep in mind that the data you insert by running the query must conform to the design of the destination table. After you designate a query as an append query, Access adds the Append To row to the query design grid. Based on the table you are appending records to, Access selects and displays a matching field in the Append To row. You can change the matching fields that Access provides, but the data type and other properties of the field specified in the Append To row must be compatible with the field in the query. The source data must also conform to any validation rules defined for the destination table or the fields that the table contains.

As with make-table queries, you create an append query by first defining a select query. After setting up the select query, verify that it returns the records you need by running it. If the results are correct, you can then select the table you want to append records to.

Action queries can also be used to update or delete records. For example, you can use an update query to increase the values in a price field by a specified percentage or to perform date arithmetic by adding or subtracting a specific time period to the values in a date field. A delete query removes the set of records that meets criteria you define. You can use a delete query to remove all products marked Discontinued, for example.

To create an update query or a delete query, you start by creating a select query. For an update query, Access adds the Update To row to the design grid and removes the Sort and Show rows. In the Update To row for the field or fields you want to modify, you enter the expression that will update the field's current values. For example, to add 30 days to the ExpirationDate field, you would enter the expression *[ExpirationDate]+30*. When you run the update query, Access displays a message box telling you how many rows (records) will be updated.

> **IMPORTANT** You cannot undo the changes made by an update query or a delete query. Before you run the query, you should make a backup copy of the table whose records will be updated or deleted. You can check which records will be affected before you run the query by switching the query to Datasheet view.

In a delete query, Access adds the Delete row to the query grid and removes the Show and Sort rows. In the Delete row, the keyword *Where* appears. Specify criteria in the Criteria row that selects the records Access will delete. For example, you might delete all records where the Discontinued field equals Yes or all task records for which the status is marked as complete.

When you work with delete queries, you might delete records you weren't expecting to. This occurs if the table you're deleting records from is related to another table, and the tables' relationship is set up to use the Cascade Delete Related Records option. You can turn off this option if necessary by modifying the tables' relationship.

> **See Also** For more information about the Cascade Delete Related Records option, see "Objective 1.2: Manage relationships and keys."

To create and run a make-table query

1. Create a select query on which to base the make-table query.

   > **See Also** For more information about how to create a select query, see "Create select queries" earlier in this topic.

2. With the select query open in Design view, on the **Design** tool tab, in the **Results** group, click **Run**.

3. Review the records returned by the select query in Datasheet view.

4. On the **Home** tab, in the **Views** group, click **View**, and then click **Design View** to return the query to Design view.

5. On the **Design** tool tab, in the **Query Type** group, click **Make Table**.

6. In the **Make Table** dialog box, enter a name for the table, and then do one of the following:

   - To have Access create the table in the current database, click **Current Database**.

   - To have Access create the table in another database, click **Another Database**. Then either enter the file name in the **File Name** box, or click **Browse**, navigate to and select the file, and then click **OK** to return to the Make Table dialog box.

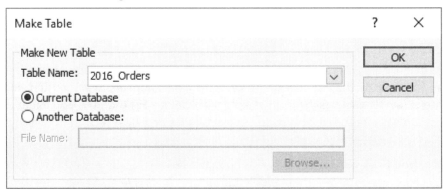

Options for running a make table query

7. Click **OK** to close the Make Table dialog box.

8. On the **Design** tool tab, in the **Results** group, click **Run**.

9. In the **Microsoft Access** message box alerting you that you'll be pasting rows into a new table and the operation can't be undone, click **Yes**.

To create and run an append query

1. Create a select query on which to base the append query.

   > **See Also** For more information about how to create a select query, see "Create select queries" earlier in this topic.

2. With the select query open in Design view, on the **Design** tool tab, in the **Results** group, click **Run**.

3. Review the records returned by the select query in Datasheet view.

4. On the **Home** tab, in the **Views** group, click **View**, and then click **Design View** to return the query to Design view.

5. On the **Design** tool tab, in the **Query Type** group, click **Append** to open the Append dialog box.

6. If you want to add the records to a table in a different database, click **Another Database**, and then either enter the database name in the **File Name** box, or click **Browse**, navigate to and select the file, and then click **OK**.

7. In the **Append** dialog box, expand the **Table Name** list and click the table you want to add the records to. Then click **OK**.

8. On the **Design** tool tab, in the **Results** group, click **Run**.

9. In the **Microsoft Access** dialog box asking you to confirm the operation, click **Yes**.

To create and run an update query

1. Create a select query on which to base the update query.

   > **See Also** For more information about how to create a select query, see "Create select queries" earlier in this topic.

2. On the **Design** tool tab, in the **Query Type** group, click **Update**.

3. In the **Update To** row for the field or fields you want to update, enter an expression that calculates the updated values.

4. On the **Design** tool tab, in the **Results** group, click **Run**.

5. In the **Microsoft Access** dialog box asking you to confirm the operation, click **Yes**.

To create and run a delete query

1. Create a select query on which to base the delete query.

   > **See Also** For more information about how to create a select query, see "Create select queries" earlier in this topic.

2. On the **Design** tool tab, in the **Query Type** group, click **Delete**.

3. In the **Criteria** row, specify the criteria for selecting the records you want to delete.

4. On the **Design** tool tab, in the **Results** group, click **Run**.

5. In the **Microsoft Access** dialog box asking you to confirm the operation, click **Yes**.

Create multiple-table queries

You can create a multiple-table query to return a set of records from related tables or from tables you join for the query itself. For example, you can join the Customers table to the Orders table by using the CustomerID field.

Whenever you have relationships defined between two tables, Access automatically joins the tables by using the fields in the defined relationships. Access also includes an option named Enable AutoJoin. This option is enabled by default, so when you create a query that includes tables that aren't directly related, Access tries to link the tables for you by examining the primary key fields for each table and then looking for a field with the same name and data type in one of the other tables in the query. If Access doesn't find a match, you can link the tables yourself. By joining the tables in this way, you link them for the purposes of designing and running the query. You don't create a permanent table relationship.

Tip You can manage the Enable AutoJoin feature from the Object Designers page of the Access Options dialog box.

See Also For more information about table relationships, see "Objective 1.2: Manage relationships and keys."

To retrieve the records you need in a query, you use either an inner join or an outer join. The default join is an inner join. With an inner join, a query returns only records with matching rows in both tables. For example, a query that joins a projects table and a tasks table returns records only for projects that have assigned tasks, and for tasks that are assigned to specific projects. By using an outer join in this query, you can retrieve the set of matching records (projects and their assigned tasks) in addition to projects without tasks (all projects) or tasks without projects (all tasks).

You can create a "left" outer join or a "right" outer join to retrieve all the records from one of the tables. *Left* and *right* refer to how the tables are identified in the Join Properties dialog box. Access provides options to create an outer join that returns all records from one table and matching records from another, depending on which table's records you want to view.

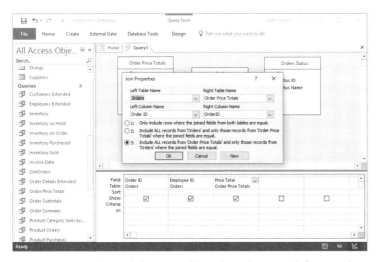

Outer joins return all records from one table and matching records from another

---

Tip You can also specify the join type that related tables use when you have the Relationships window open. Click the relationship line for the tables you want to work with, and then click Edit Relationships in the Tools group on the Relationship Tools Design tool tab. Click Join Type in the Edit Relationships dialog box, and then click the option for the type of join you want to use.

To add tables to a query

→ In the **Query Designer**, right-click an empty area of the main pane (not on a field list), and then click **Show Table**.

Or

1. Open the query in Design view.
2. On the **Design** tool tab, in the **Query Setup** group, click **Show Table**.
3. In the **Show Table** dialog box, select the tables or queries you want to add, click **Add**, and then click **Close**.

To remove a table from a query

1. Open the query in Design view.
2. Right-click the field list for the table, and then click **Remove Table**.

To set up an outer join for tables in a query

1. In the **Query Designer**, right-click the line that links the tables, and then click **Join Properties**.
2. In the **Join Properties** dialog box, click one of the following options, and then click **OK**:

   - To include only rows where the joined fields from both tables are equal, click option **1**.

   - To include all records from the left table and only matching records from the right table, click option **2**.

   - To include all records from the right table and only matching records from the left table, click option **3**.

Save queries

Access automatically saves a query you create by using one of the query wizards. The wizard provides a default name for the query based on the first (or only) table or query you select as the query's data source. When you design a query in the Query Designer, Access assigns a default name such as *Query1*. You can replace either default name with a more meaningful one. You cannot use the same name for a table and a query. To avoid this conflict, you can include a prefix such as *qry* in each query's name.

You can use options on the Save As page in the Backstage view to create a copy of a query as a new database object (a new query, form, or report) or as a PDF or an XPS file. Saving a query as a new database object can be helpful if you want to experiment with the query by adding additional selection criteria, for example, but don't want to risk inadvertent changes to the original query. A form or report you create by saving a query as a database object contains the query's fields and provides a starting point from which you can further develop the object you create. When you save a query as a PDF or an XPS file, you create a static copy of the query's data. You can specify a range of pages to save and also set accessibility options.

When you delete a query from a database, keep in mind that queries are often used as the record source for forms and reports. If you delete a query that is the basis of a form or report, you must update the record source before you can use the form or report to view records.

To save a query from Design view

1. On the **Quick Access Toolbar**, click **Save**.

2. In the **Save As** dialog box, enter a name for the query, and then click **OK**.

To save a query as a database object

1. In the **Navigation Pane**, right-click the query, and then click **Open**.

2. Click the **File** tab, and then click **Save As.**

3. In the **File Types** list, click **Save Object As**.

4. In the **Save the current database object** area, under **Database File Types**, click **Save Object As**, and then click **Save As**.

5. In the **Save As** dialog box, in the **Save *QueryName* to** box, enter a name for the query.

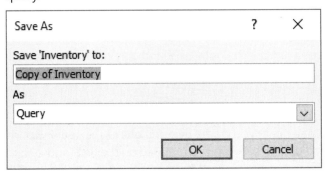

Saving a query as a new database object

6. In the **As** box, select **Query**, **Form**, or **Report**.

7. Click **OK**.

To save a query as a PDF or XPS file

1. In the **Navigation Pane**, right-click the query, and then click **Open**.

2. Click the **File** tab, and then click **Save As**.

3. In the **File Types** list, click **Save Object As**.

4. In the **Save the current database object** area, under **Database File Types**, click **PDF or XPS**, and then click **Save As**.

5. In the **Publish as PDF or XPS** dialog box, in the **File name** box, modify the name Access supplies if necessary.

6. In the **Save as type** list, select **PDF** or **XPS Document**.

7. To set a page range or other options, click **Options**, specify the options you want to use, and then click **OK** in the **Options** dialog box.

8. In the **Publish as PDF or XPS** dialog box, click **Publish**.

3

Objective 3.1 practice tasks

The practice file for these tasks is located in the **MOSAccess2016\Objective3** practice file folder. The folder also contains a result file that you can use to check your work.

➤ Open the **Access_3-1** database and do the following:

❑ Use the Simple Query Wizard to create a detail query that contains all the fields in the CampaignExpenses table. Name the query MOSAccess_Query1. Choose the option to view information so that you can examine the query's results.

❑ Close MOSAccess_Query1.

❑ Use the Query Designer to create a select query based on the MarketingCampaigns table. Add the fields CampaignID, Country, and CampaignBudget. Save the query as MOSAccess_Query2. Convert this query to an update query to increase campaign budgets by 10 percent. Close the query.

❑ Use the Query Designer to create a select query based on the CampaignExpenses, CampaignExpenseTypes, and MarketingCampaigns tables. Add the CampaignID and Country fields from the MarketingCampaign table, the ExpenseType field from the CampaignExpenseTypes table, and the AmountSpent field from the CampaignExpenses table. Save the query as MOSAccess_Query3. Run the query to display the records returned by the select query. Now convert this query to a crosstab query. Use the AmountSpent field as the value field. Use the Country field as the row heading field and the ExpenseType field as the column heading field. Select Sum in the Total row for the AmountSpent field.

❑ Open the Tasks query in Design view.

❑ Open the Show Table dialog box, and add the MarketingCampaigns table to the query.

❑ From the MarketingCampaigns table, add the Country field to the query, and then run the query to display the results.

❑ Open the Show Table dialog box again, and add the Employees table to the query. Remove the MarketingCampaigns table from the Query Designer.

❑ Join the Tasks and the Employees tables by using the EmployeeID and AssignedTo fields.

❑ Add the AssignedTo field to the query, and then run the query to review the results. Use the options in the Join Properties dialog box to create an outer join that shows all the records from the Tasks table. Run the query again to view how the outer join changes the query's results.

➤ Open the **Access_3-1_results** database. Compare the two databases to check your work. Then close the open databases.

Objective 3.2: Modify queries

After you set up a query, you can modify it by renaming it, changing or rearranging the fields, showing and hiding query fields, and sorting the query's results. You can also format the fields in a query. This topic examines some of the ways you can modify a query.

Rename queries

Renaming a query can affect database objects that use the query as a record source. If you rename a query that is the record source for a report, for example, but don't change the Record Source property for the report, Access can't open the report.

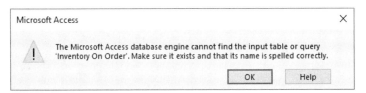

Renaming a query can prevent Access from opening an object that depends on the query

By default, Access sets two Name AutoCorrect options for managing objects that you rename. With these options selected, when you rename a query, Access updates the name of the query automatically in other objects where it is used as a record source.

See Also For more information about the Name AutoCorrect options, see "Objective 2.2: Manage tables."

To rename a query

1. In the **Navigation Pane**, right-click the query, and then click **Rename**.

2. Enter a new name for the query, and then click away from the Navigation Pane.

Change the fields in a query

With a query open in Design view, you can add, remove, and rearrange the query's fields in several ways. To add fields, you can use the field list or the Field row in the design grid. When you drag a field between two fields already in the grid, Access moves the other fields in the query to the right. You can also use the options in the

Show Table dialog box to add another table or query to the query and then include fields from those objects in the query's design. When you remove a field, you cannot use the Undo command to reverse this action.

You can also reposition the fields in a query design grid.

To add fields to a query

1. Open the query in Design view.

2. Do either of the following:

   - In the field list in the top pane of the **Query Designer**, select the field, and then drag the field to the query design grid.

   - In the **Field** row in a blank column in the design grid, select the field you want to add.

To delete a field

→ In the design grid, click the field column header, and then press **Delete**.

To insert a column in the design grid

1. In the query design grid, click in the column that you want to insert a new column to the left of.

2. On the **Design** tool tab, in the **Query Setup** group, click **Insert Column.**

To delete a column in the design grid

1. In the query design grid, click in the column that you want to delete.

2. On the **Design** tool tab, in the **Query Setup** group, click **Delete Column.**

To change the order of the fields in the design grid

→ Click the top of the column for the field you want to move (hold down the **Shift** key to select more than one column), and then drag the column or columns to the new location.

3

Show and hide query fields

By default, the check box in the Show row for each field in a query is selected. This means that the values in each field are displayed in the query's results. By clearing this check box for a field, you remove that field's values from the query's result without removing the field from the query.

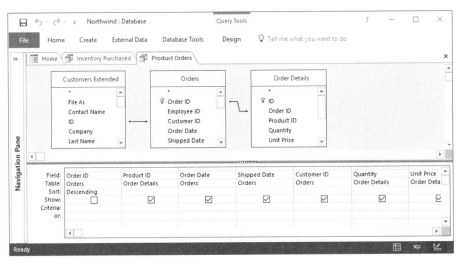

Access shows only those fields selected in the Show row

The capability to hide a field is helpful when you want to use a field to define selection criteria or to sort a query but don't want to show the field in the query's results. Fields you use this way are essential to defining the query, but their values don't need to be shown in the query's results. You might add an ID field or a date field to a query for these purposes. For the ID field, you might specify a customer's ID. You could use the date field to sort records to display orders sequentially since the start of your fiscal year. The purpose of these fields is to tailor the query—any reporting or analysis doesn't require that the query include the values that these fields provide.

To show and hide query fields

1. Open the query in Design view.

2. In the query design grid, clear the **Show** check box for any fields you want to hide.

3. Select the **Show** check box to display a field in the results.

Specify the sort order for queries

You use the Sort row in the query design grid to specify how Access sorts the records returned by a query. You can sort by a single field or by more than one field. When you specify a sort order for more than one field, Access sorts records according to the order in which the fields appear left to right in the query design grid.

Tip If you add all the fields from a table or query to the query design grid by dragging the asterisk, you cannot use the Sort row to sort records.

If you want to sort by multiple fields in a specific sequence but also display one of these fields later in the order of the fields, you can add a second instance of the field, set the sort order for the field, and then hide the second instance of the field so that it doesn't appear in the query's results.

The sorting options are Ascending, Descending, and Not Sorted. Be sure to reposition fields as you want them to appear when you are sorting records by more than one field.

See Also For more information about how to rearrange field order, see "Change the fields in a query" earlier in this topic.

To use the Sort row in a query

1. Open the query in Design view.

2. In the query design grid, click in the **Sort** row for the field you want to sort by, click the arrow, and then select **Ascending**, **Descending**, or **Not Sorted**.

3. To sort by more than one field, specify the sort order for the additional fields. In the query design grid, arrange the fields from left to right in the order you want Access to use them to sort records.

Format fields in a query

At times, you might want to print the results of a query or save the results as a PDF file for distribution. To enhance the plain display of the query's results in the datasheet, you can apply text formatting. For example, you can display or hide gridlines, apply a different background color to alternate rows, select a different font and font size, and apply font attributes such as bold or italic.

The text formatting you apply affects all the records in a query. You can't, for example, apply bold formatting to only one column of values in the query's datasheet. Adding or modifying alternate row colors and displaying gridlines help distinguish the rows and columns of data.

In a query, you can use a field's Format property to display the values in that field differently from the way the field's format is specified in the table in which the field is defined. For example, a date field can be defined with the Short Date format in its table but displayed in the Long Date format in a query. You can also use a field's Caption property in a query to display a different label in the column heading. Setting the Format or Caption property for a field in a query does not define or change the property for the field in its table.

To apply text formatting to a query

1. Open the query in Datasheet view.

2. On the **Home** tab, in the **Text Formatting** group, do any of the following:

   - In the **Font**, **Font Size**, or **Font Color** lists, select a different font, font size, or font color.

   - Click the **Bold**, **Italic**, or **Underline** buttons to format the text.

   - Click the **Background Color** arrow, and then select a background color for odd-numbered rows.

   - Click the **Gridlines** arrow, and then select to show both horizontal and vertical gridlines, only horizontal gridlines, only vertical gridlines, or no gridlines.

   - Click the **Alternate Row Color** arrow, and select a color that is applied to even-numbered rows.

To set properties for a field in a query

1. Open the query in Design view.

2. On the **Design** tool tab, in the **Show/Hide** group, click **Property Sheet**.

3. Click in the column for the field you want to format.

4. In the property sheet, enter or select a value for properties such as **Format** and **Caption**.

Objective 3.2 practice tasks

The practice file for these tasks is located in the **MOSAccess2016 \Objective3** practice file folder. The folder also contains a result file that you can use to check your work.

➤ Open the **Access_3-2** database.

➤ Open the TaskAssignments query in Design view, and make the following changes. Run the query after each change to check how the change affects the query's results.

❑ From the Tasks table, add the TaskName, Description, Start Date, and Due Date fields to the query.

❑ Hide the Task ID field.

❑ Sort the query in ascending order on the Start Date field.

❑ Set the Caption property for the AssignedTo field to Current Assignment.

❑ Open the query in Datasheet view.

❑ Apply the *Blue, Accent 1* theme color as the alternating row color.

❑ Save and close the query.

➤ Open the **Access_3-2_results** database. Compare the two databases to check your work. Then close the open databases.

Objective 3.3: Create calculated fields and grouping within queries

In addition to using a query to select records and perform operations such as updating, deleting, or appending records, you can filter the records in a query and use queries to summarize and group data. For example, you can use a query to show the average value in a field or to count the number of records that meet specific criteria. This section provides examples of how to group and summarize records in a query. It also describes how to create a calculated field—a field whose data is derived from the values in other fields but not stored in the database itself—and how to group data by using some of the operators that Access provides.

Use calculated fields

You use expressions in many areas of Access—in validation rules, for example. Expressions contain several elements, including functions, operators, constants, and identifiers (which refer to the names of fields or tables, for example).

Expressions are used in queries to define criteria and can also be used to create calculated fields. For example, in a query that summarizes orders, you can use an expression to create a calculated field that shows the period of time between the order date and the date the order was shipped. This expression would look like the following:

[OrderDate]-[ShippedDate]

When you use an expression to create a calculated field, Access provides the default label *Expr1* (for the first expression in a query) as a column heading in the results datasheet. To name the calculated field, you can enter the field name you want to use followed by a colon and the expression—for example:

Fulfillment Time:[OrderDate]-[ShippedDate]

Identifiers such as field names are enclosed in square brackets. Here's another example of a calculated field, which uses the IIf and Date functions to define a conditional expression that indicates whether an invoice is past due.

Invoice Status:IIf([Invoice Date]<Date()-30,"Past Due", "On Track")

The expression in this calculated field checks the value in the Invoice Date field, and if that date is more than 30 days past the current date (calculated by the Date function), it displays Past Due in the calculated field. If the invoice date is earlier than 30 days from today, the calculated field displays On Track.

You can enter an expression directly in the Field row or use the Zoom dialog box or the Expression Builder to help you create the expression. The Zoom dialog box provides a large text box in which you can compose an expression. You can also select a different font, font style, font size, and other attributes. Access doesn't display this formatting in the Query Designer, but the formatting might improve the readability of the expression while you are working with it in the Zoom dialog box.

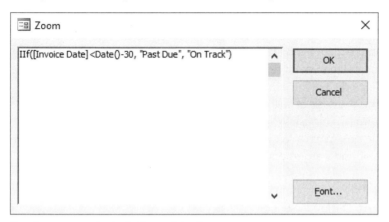

Entering an expression in the Zoom dialog box

The Expression Builder provides lists of database objects, fields, values, and other elements you include in an expression. You can enter the expression in the top pane or select options in the Expression Elements, Expression Categories, and Expression Values panes. The Expression Values pane is blank until you select an option other than the current object in the Expression Elements pane.

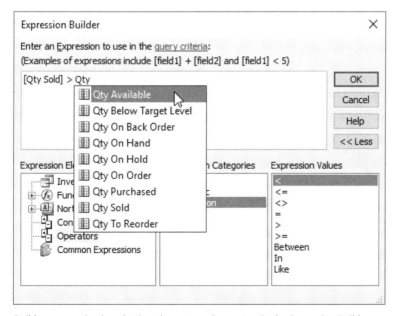

Build an expression by selecting elements and operators in the Expression Builder

You build an expression by selecting items in the three bottom panes. In most cases, you build expressions from left to right. When you select an element in the Expression Elements list, the categories for that element appear in the Expression Categories pane. When you select a category, the Expression Builder lists the values related to that category in the Expression Values pane.

When you enter text in the main pane of the Expression Builder, Access displays a list of items that match the characters you enter. You can choose a function name or a field name from this list to include it in the expression. As you continue entering characters, Access adjusts the list on the basis of each character you enter. Access might also display a description of the items in this list. When you select a function from the list or start entering a function's name, Access also provides information about the function's syntax, showing required and optional arguments.

To create a calculated field

1. Open the query in Design view.

2. In the **Query Designer**, click in the **Field** row in the column in which you want to insert the calculated field.

3. Enter the label you want to use before the expression, followed by a colon, and then enter the expression that performs the calculation.

To display the Zoom dialog box

1. In the query design grid, click in the cell where you want to write an expression—for example, a cell in the **Field** or **Criteria** row.

2. Press **Shift+F2**.

To open the Expression Builder

→ In the **Query Designer**, right-click in the **Field** or **Criteria** row, and then click **Build**.

→ On the **Design** tool tab, in the **Query Setup** group, click **Build**.

Set filter criteria

A select query often includes criteria that defines the subset of records the query returns when you run it. For example, to find records for customers in a specific city, you can add the City field to the query and then enter an expression such as *="CityName"* (where *"CityName"* is the city you want to examine) to the Criteria row. You must enclose text values in quotation marks.

To specify criteria for a date field, enclose the date (or dates) in pound signs (#). You can retrieve records for orders placed between two dates by using an expression such as *Between #4/1/2017# and #6/30/2017#*. You can also use comparison operators to retrieve records that are less than (<) or greater than (>) a certain numeric amount.

See Also For more information about the operators you can use in a query, see "Group data by using operators" later in this topic.

When you enter criteria in the Criteria row for more than one field, the query selects only records that match the criteria in all those fields—for example, records that have a value in the Order Date field greater than 9/15/2017 and a value of Fabrikam for the Company Name field. You can set up OR criteria (to find records with a value of Fabrikam or Contoso in the Company Name field, for example) by entering the second criteria in the Or row (below the Criteria row).

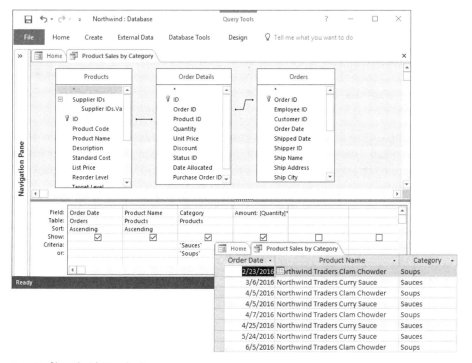

A query filtered with Or criteria

You can filter the results of a query in Datasheet view by applying the filtering tools and options available for filtering records in a table.

See Also For more information about filtering results, see "Find, sort, and filter data," in "Objective 2.3: Manage records in tables."

To set filter criteria

1. In the query design grid, click in the **Criteria** row for the field you want to filter by.

2. Enter the expression for the criteria you want to apply to the field.

3. To define criteria for more than one field, do either of the following:

   - To apply And criteria, click in the **Criteria** row for another field, and then enter the expression to use as a filter.

   - To apply Or criteria, click in the **Or** row for another field, and then enter the expression to use as a filter.

4. Run the query to display the results.

Group and summarize query records

When you set up and run a query in Design view, Access by default creates a detail query that returns each record that matches the query's fields and any criteria you define. For example, a query designed to show sales in each category by order date will display all the individual orders placed on a specific date. In a case like this, how-ever, you can gain another perspective on the data by displaying the total ordered for each category on a specific date instead of the amounts for each individual order. To perform an operation such as this in a query, you use the Total row.

Access displays the Group By option in the Total row when you insert the row. On its own, this option returns records that have unique values in each field in the query. You can use the Group By option together with a summary function to summarize data. For example, without settings specified in the Total row, Access would display a record for each order when you run the query. After displaying the Total row and specifying the Sum function for the Quantity field, the query displays the quantity ordered in each category on a specific day.

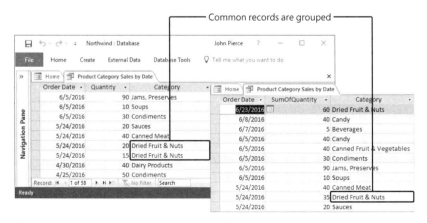

A summary query groups and summarizes records

In addition to Sum, you can apply various other functions to the data in a summary query. The options in the Total row also include the following functions:

- **Avg** This calculates the average of the values in the field.

- **Min** This identifies the smallest value in the field.

- **Max** This identifies the largest value in the field.

- **Count** This counts the number of values in a field, but ignores Null (blank) values.

- **StDev** This shows you the standard deviation for the values in the field.

- **Var** This calculates the variance of the values in the field.

- **First** This returns the value for the field from the first row encountered in the group.

- **Last** This returns the value for the field from the last row encountered in the group.

- **Expression** Select this option when you want to create an expression in the Total row that uses one or more of the aggregate functions Access provides.

- **Where** Use this setting to apply a filter to the records in the query.

To display several summary values for a specific field at one time, add several instances of the field to the query and then choose a different summary function for each instance. For example, you could add three instances of the Quantity field to display the total quantity ordered in addition to the minimum and maximum quantities.

When you create a totals query, Access appends the name of the summary function to the field name and displays labels such as *AvgOfQuantity*. You can create your own labels in the Query Designer by entering the text you want to use in front of the field name in the Field row, followed by a colon. For example, instead of using *AvgOfQuantity*, you could enter <u>Average Quantity:</u> in front of the field name *Quantity*. Access uses this label when you display the query results in Datasheet view.

You can apply criteria to a summary query to select specific records. For example, when you use the Sum function in the Total row, enter a value in the Criteria row to select values that are above or below a certain threshold—to select total quantities greater than 250, for example, you would enter <u>>250</u>.

To group records in a query

1. Open the query in Design view.
2. On the **Design** tool tab, in the **Show/Hide** group, click **Totals**.
3. In the **Total** row, specify the settings you want for grouping fields.

To view summary data in a query

1. Open the query in Design view.

2. On the **Design** tool tab, in the **Show/Hide** group, click **Totals**.

3. In the **Total** row, select the summary function you want to apply to a field.

4. Use the **Criteria** row to define criteria you want to apply to the summary query.

5. To apply a filter to the query, select **Where** in the **Total** row, and then specify the filter criteria in the **Criteria** row.

6. On the **Design** tool tab, in the **Results** group, click **Run** to display the query results.

Group data by using operators

Throughout this chapter are examples of different operators you can use in expressions that define query criteria, filters, or calculated fields. The operators you can use include basic arithmetic operators for addition (+), subtraction (–), multiplication (/), and division (*). You can use the ampersand (&) to combine the values in two or more text fields. For example, the expression *[City] & ", " & [State/Province]* combines the City and State/Province fields in a single text string.

Access also provides logical operators, such as Or, And, and Not, and comparison operators, such as < (less than) and > (greater than). Here are a few examples of how to use these operators in criteria expressions.

Expression	Result
<Date()	Returns records with a date earlier than the current date
"Lee" or "Andersen"	Returns records with either Lee or Andersen as the value in the field
Not "Andersen"	Returns records except those with Andersen as the value in the field
Not <#4/1/2017#	Returns only records with a date later than 4/1/2017
<=50	Returns records with a value of 50 or less
<>"Beverages"	Returns records that do not equal Beverages in this field

Three other comparison operators are Like, In, and Between. The Like operator can be used to compare a field value to a text string. For example, the expression *Like "98###"* in a postal code field returns records with ZIP Code values that start with 98. You can use the In operator to find specific records. The expression *In ("Las Vegas")* returns records with the value *Las Vegas* in the city field. Use the Between operator to select records within a range of dates (*Between #1/1/2017# And #3/31/2017#*) or a range of numbers (*Between 1200 And 1500*).

You can use these operators in expressions you apply to a summary query that groups data. For example, in a query designed to analyze expenses, you could use the < > operator to exclude records for expenses in categories you don't need to review, the Between operator to specify a date range, and the expression *"USA" or "France"* to select the countries or regions you are interested in.

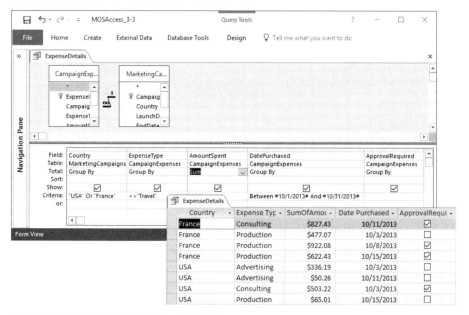

A summary query using operators to group data

Objective 3.3 practice tasks

The practice file for these tasks is located in the **MOSAccess2016\Objective3** practice file folder. The folder also contains a result file that you can use to check your work.

➤ Open the **Access_3-3** database and do the following:

- ❑ Open the CampaignExpenseSummary query in Design view.
- ❑ Add a Total row to the query, and summarize the AmountSpent field by using the Sum function, Min function, and Max function.
- ❑ From the MarketingCampaigns table, add the CampaignBudget field to the query, and then save the query.
- ❑ Create a calculated field that divides the AmountSpent field by the CampaignBudget field. Create a label for the calculated field named <u>Percent of Budget</u>. Use the query property sheet to apply the Percent format to this field, using two decimal places.
- ❑ Hide the CampaignBudget field, and then run the query to display the results.
- ❑ Save and close the CampaignExpenseSummary query.
- ❑ Open the ExpenseDetails query in Design view.
- ❑ Add a Total row to the query, and select the Sum function for the AmountSpent field.
- ❑ Using operators, add criteria that returns expenses records after 10/15/2016 for the categories Production and Consulting, excluding records for the United States.

➤ Open the **Access_3-3_results** database. Compare the two databases to check your work. Then close the open databases.

Objective group 4
Create forms

The skills tested in this section of the Microsoft Office Specialist exam for Microsoft Access 2016 relate to building forms. Specifically, the following objectives are associated with this set of skills:

4.1 Create forms

4.2 Configure form controls

4.3 Format forms

Forms are often based on one or more of the tables and queries in an Access database. Forms serve as a user interface for the database, simplifying how you navigate between objects, records, and features and helping you organize the work of inserting and updating data.

When you create forms, you can work with a wizard or build the form from scratch by working in Design view or Layout view. You build a form by adding controls, including text boxes and lists boxes that correspond to fields in the form's data source and command buttons that perform operations such as opening another form. Access provides tools that you can use to manage the size, position, alignment, and other properties of a form's controls. In addition, you can format a form so that it displays an image or displays the records in a specific sort order.

This chapter guides you in studying ways of creating forms, configuring form controls, and formatting forms.

4

To complete the practice tasks in this chapter, you need the practice files contained in the **MOSAccess2016\Objective4** practice file folder. For more information, see "Download the practice files" in this book's introduction.

Objective 4.1: Create forms

You can create a fully functioning form in a single step, you can use the Form Wizard, or you can create a blank form and then place and define each element of the form yourself. When you design a form yourself, you work in Design view or Layout view.

Access also provides application parts that serve as form templates, and tools for creating forms that use a specific layout, including a navigation form.

See Also For more information about creating a navigation form, see "Objective 1.3: Navigate through a database."

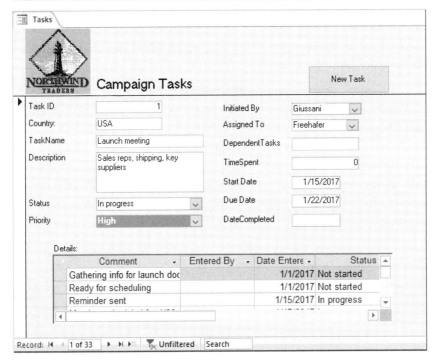

A complete form with a subform showing details

You work with several elements in forms. Forms use controls to display data (a text box or a list box, for example), to identify information (label controls), to aid navigation (hyperlinks and button controls), and to organize and emphasize aspects of a form's layout (line and rectangle controls). Both a form and its controls use properties to define their data source, their size and position, their format, and other aspects of their appearance and behavior. When you use a wizard to create a form, the wizard sets most properties to default values. You can adjust these settings in the form property sheet and by using commands on the ribbon.

See Also For more information about form properties, see "Set control properties," in "Objective 4.2: Configure form controls."

This topic describes various ways to create a form, including by using a wizard, from scratch, and from a template. It also describes how to save a form.

Create quick forms

The fastest way to create a form is to select a table or query in the Navigation Pane and then use the Form command in the Forms group on the Create tab. Access creates a form that includes all the fields in the table or query (which serves as the form's record source) and displays the form in Layout view. You can use a form you create by using the Form command to work with one record at a time or modify the form by adding other controls, changing formatting, and defining features.

See Also For information about adding and formatting form controls, see "Objective 4.2: Configure form controls."

The More Forms menu includes four entries that you can also use to create a quick form:

- **Multiple Items** Lists multiple records at the same time.
- **Datasheet** Shows records in a datasheet.
- **Split Form** Creates a form that includes a datasheet in the top portion and a form designed for data entry in the bottom portion.
- **Modal Dialog** Creates a dialog box that is displayed until a user takes an action. You can use a modal dialog as a navigation form, for example. The Modal Dialog option is not based on a table or query that you select in the Navigation Pane. You need to design this form from scratch.

See Also For information, see "Create forms from scratch," later in this topic.

4

To create a quick form

1. In the **Navigation Pane**, select the table or query you want to use as the form record source.

2. On the **Create** tab, in the **Forms** group, do either of the following:

   - Click **Form** to create a form that displays a single record from the record source.

   - Click **More Forms**, and then select the type of form you want to create: **Multiple Items**, **Datasheet**, **Split Form**, or **Modal Dialog**.

Create forms by using the Form Wizard

You can build a form almost as quickly—and gain options for selecting fields and a form layout—by using the Form Wizard. The Form Wizard uses the table or query selected in the Navigation Pane as the default choice for the form's record source. You can choose a different object or add fields from additional tables or queries.

The Form Wizard offers four layout options: Columnar, Tabular, Datasheet, and Justified. When you select a layout, the wizard shows a preview of what the form will look like.

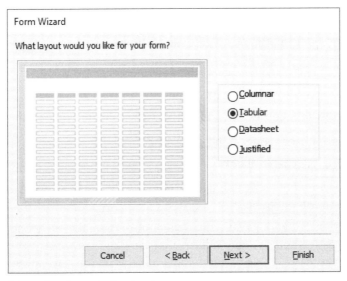

Select a form layout in the wizard

Access assigns a default name to the form and prompts you to either open the form to work with data or open the form in Design view to modify it.

To create a form by using the Form Wizard

1. On the **Create** tab, in the **Forms** group, click **Form Wizard**.

2. On the first page of the **Form Wizard**, select the table or query you want to use as the form's record source.

3. Move the fields you want to include on the form from the **Available Fields** list to the **Selected Fields** list, and then click **Next**.

4. Choose a layout for the form. Use the previews that the wizard displays when you select a layout option to view the form's general appearance.

5. Enter a name for the form (or accept the default name), and then specify whether you want to open the form to view and update data or open the form in Design view to modify the form.

6. Click **Finish** to create the form.

Create forms from scratch

When you create a form from scratch, you can open the new form in Design view or Layout view. In either view, you start with a blank form window and the field list. In the field list, you can expand an entry for a table to view the fields that table contains. After you add a field to the form, Access updates the field list, dividing it into three areas:

- **Fields available for this view** This area shows the fields from the table you selected as the record source.

- **Fields available in related tables** This area lists the tables related to the table that is serving as the form's record source.

4

- **Fields available in other tables** This area lists the other tables in the database. (If all the tables in the database are related to the table you are using, Access does not display this group.)

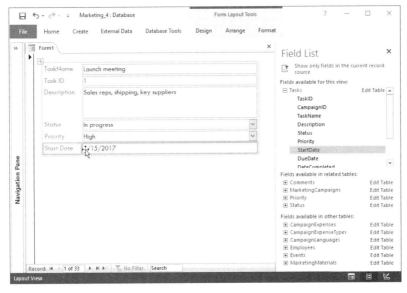

Creating a form in Layout view

By default, the fields you add to a form in Layout view are stacked in columns. Each field's label appears in a column on the left, and the field's input control (a text box or a list box, for example) appears on the right. When you drag a field from the field list to the form, Access displays an orange bar at the bottom of the stack; you can drag up to insert the field between fields already on the form. You can insert a column or a row to the layout as you refine the form's design.

See Also For more information about moving controls on a form, see "Move controls" in "Objective 4.2: Configure form controls."

The field list includes links that you can use to change which fields it displays and to work with data. Clicking the Show Only Fields In The Current Record Source link at the top of the field list displays only those fields you have added to the form. The Edit Table links (which appear to the right of a table's name) open a table in Datasheet view, where you can view, insert, or update data while you are designing the form.

When you add a field to a form, Access uses the field's data type to determine which type of form control to associate with the field. In many cases (for text and number fields, for example), Access creates a text box control and an associated label. For lookup fields, Access creates a combo box control, and for Yes/No fields, Access inserts a check box control. You can add other types of controls—a command button, for example, or a label control—by using the options in the Controls group on the Design tool tab.

One of the main advantages of working in Layout view is that Access displays data from the underlying record source as you design the form. In Design view, you don't see live data and controls are not aligned in a set layout, but you do see a design grid and have greater flexibility for where you can place individual controls.

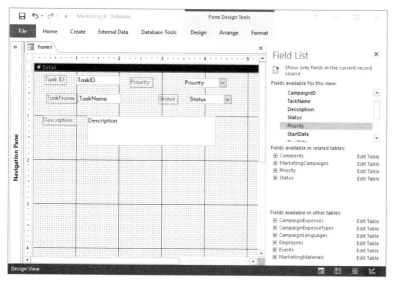

Creating a form in Design view

The tools and methods you use to create a form in Design view are similar to those you work with in Layout view. You can expand the list of fields for the table you want to use as the form's record source and drag fields to place them on the form. When you add the first field to the form, Access updates the fields displayed in the field list as it does in Layout view. To align and position fields when you work in Design view, use the grid marks and the ruler. Access highlights the ruler when you drag a control and shows the control's position relative to other controls. By right-clicking a control, you can work with the options on the Align, Size, and Position menus to adjust the layout of the form.

When you first create a form in Design view, the form contains only the Detail section. You locate most of the form's controls in its Detail section, but a form can also include a Header and a Footer section. You can use the Header section to display the form's title, to include a logo, or to show the date and time, for example. You might use the Footer section to show a Totals field that is calculated from the values of other fields on the form.

> **See Also** For more information about form headers and footers, see "Insert form headers and footers" in "Objective 4.3: Format forms." For more information about adding form controls and setting control properties, see "Add and remove controls" and "Set control properties" in "Objective 4.2: Configure form controls."

Part of creating a form is setting the form's properties. A form and its sections (Form Header, Detail, and Form Footer) have numerous properties you can set and modify in the form property sheet. With the property sheet open, you can select Detail, Form Header, or Form Footer from the Selection Type list to view and set properties for that section. Select Form to work with the properties for the form itself.

For a form, you might work with one or more of the following properties on the Format tab of the property sheet:

- **Default View** Use the Default View property to specify the view in which Access opens the form when a user double-clicks the form in the Navigation Pane or clicks Form View on the View menu. The options are Datasheet, Single Form (which displays a single record on the form), and Continuous Forms (which displays multiple records).

- **Allow Form View, Allow Datasheet View, Allow Layout View** Use these properties to control the views in which Access can display the form.

- **Navigation Buttons, Navigation Caption, Scroll Bars, Record Selectors** Set the Navigation Buttons property to No if the record navigation buttons aren't required on the form. If you do show the navigation buttons, you can enter text in the Navigation Caption property to replace the default caption *Record*. The Scroll Bars property gives you options for showing only the vertical scroll bar, only the horizontal scroll bar, both, or neither. The Record Selectors property controls whether the record selector is displayed on the form.

- **Close Button, Min Max Buttons** Set these properties to Yes or No depending on whether you want the form to include the Close, Minimize, or Maximize buttons in its upper-right corner.

On the Data tab of the property sheet, you can view and set properties that affect how a user works with the form's data.

- **Data Entry** Set this property to Yes (the default setting is No) if you want Access to display a blank record when a user opens the form.

- **Allow Additions, Allow Deletions, Allow Edits** These properties control whether a user can use this form to insert records, delete records, and change the values in form controls.
- **Allow Filters** Set this property to No if you don't want users to be able to filter the records shown in this form.

To create a form from scratch

1. On the **Create** tab, in the **Forms** group, do one of the following:
   - To open the new form in Layout view, click **Blank Form**.
   - To open the new form in Design view, click **Form Design**.
2. Display the form field list, show the tables, and expand the table you want to use as the form's record source.
3. Drag the fields you want to include on the form from the field list to the form window. You can align and reposition fields after you place them.

To open the form property sheet

1. Open the form in Design view or Layout view.
2. On the **Design** tool tab, in the **Tools** group. click **Property Sheet**.

To display the form field list

→ On the **Design** tool tab, in the **Tools** group, click **Add Existing Fields**.

To set form properties

1. Open the form property sheet.
2. At the top of the property sheet, in the **Selection type** list, click **Form**.
3. On the **Format**, **Data**, **Event**, **Other**, or **All** tab of the property sheet, locate the property you want to set.
4. Click in the property box, and then enter or select the property value you want.

4

Create forms from templates by using application parts

The Application Parts gallery provides 10 basic forms that you can use in many types of databases. The ScreenTip that Access displays when you point to an item in this gallery identifies the form's basic layout.

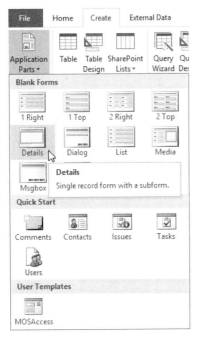

Select a basic form layout from the Application Parts gallery

When you add an application part form to a database, Access adds an entry for the form to the Navigation Pane. You can then open the form in Design view or Layout view to modify the controls that the form includes by default and to add fields and other controls.

You can create a group of forms and then save the forms as a database template, choosing the option to create an application part from the template. You could use this set of forms in multiple databases that store information of similar types and when you want the databases to have a common appearance.

See Also For more information, see "Save a database as a template," in "Objective 1.5: Print and export data."

To create a form from a template by using application parts

1. Close all open objects.

2. On the **Create** tab, in the **Templates** group, click **Application Parts**.

3. In the **Application Parts** gallery, click the form you want to add. The form appears in the Navigation Pane.

4. Open the form in Design view or Layout view to modify its content.

Save forms

Any form you create by using one of the wizards is automatically saved by Access. When you design a form from scratch in Design view or Layout view, Access assigns a default name to the form (*Form1*, for example). You can use options on the Save As page in the Backstage view to create a copy of a form as a new database object (either a form or a report) or as a PDF or an XPS file. Saving a form as a report provides a starting point for you to design a report that you can distribute to database users.

See Also For more information about saving a database object as another object, see "Save queries," in "Objective 3.1: Create queries."

To save a form

1. On the **Quick Access Toolbar**, or in the left pane of the Backstage view, click **Save**.

2. If you're saving the form for the first time, in the **Save As** dialog box, enter a name for the form, and then click **OK**.

4

Objective 4.1 practice tasks

The practice file for these tasks is located in the **MOSAccess2016\Objective4** practice file folder. The folder also contains a result file that you can use to check your work.

➤ Open the **Access_4-1** database and do the following:

❏ Use the *Form* command to create a form for the Tasks table.

❏ Save the form as <u>MyTasks</u>, and then close the form.

➤ Use the Form Wizard to do the following:

❏ Create a form based on the CampaignInfo query.

❏ Add all the fields from the query to the form.

❏ Select the option to view records by Employees by using a subform.

❏ Use the *Datasheet* layout for the subforms.

❏ Name the form <u>MyCampaigns</u>, and accept the default subform names.

➤ Complete the wizard, open the form in Design view, and then do the following:

❏ Open the property sheet, and then set the form's *Allow Additions* property to *Yes*.

❏ Save and close the form.

❏ Create a List form by using the application part templates.

❏ Open the List form in Layout view.

❏ In the form's header, replace *List Form* with <u>Budgets</u>, and then save and close the form.

➤ Open the **Access_4-1_results** database. Compare the two databases to check your work. Then close the open databases.

Objective 4.2: Configure form controls

This topic explains more about working with form controls. It describes how to move, add, and delete controls and how to work with properties that define a control's format and behavior. This section also covers how to create a subform, how to modify data sources for forms and controls, and how to manage labels.

Move controls

You can change and fine-tune a control's position in a number of ways. For example, you can drag the control or use the arrow keys to move it up, down, left, or right. The arrow keys move a control in smaller increments than dragging often affords.

By dragging a control's border, you can move the control and its label together, or you can point to the larger gray handle in a control's upper-left corner to move a label or a control independently. A control also has Top and Left properties that you can set to move a control to a precise position. The settings for the Top and Left properties position a control relative to the upper-left corner of the form.

> **See Also** For more information about control properties, see "Set control properties" later in this topic.

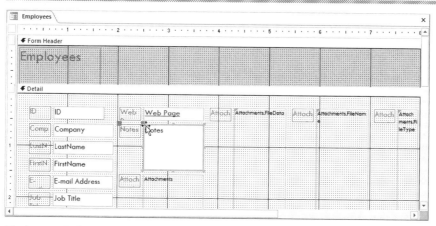

Moving a control

In Design view, you can use commands in the Sizing & Ordering group on the Arrange tab to modify the size, spacing, and alignment of controls. For example, you can make two or more text boxes the same size. You can also group controls so that you can reposition them as a unit.

Tip In the Grid section of the Size/Space menu, use the Grid command to show or hide the design grid. Temporarily hiding the grid displays the form's background more clearly. Selecting the Snap To Grid command (it is selected by default) makes positioning controls easier.

The Align command in the Sizing & Ordering group aligns a set of controls at the left, right, top, or bottom. The Left option, for example, aligns the left borders of the controls with the control farthest to the left. The Bring To Front and Send To Back commands change the relationship of objects that overlap on a form.

In Layout view, a form's controls are contained within a layout that helps manage the alignment and arrangement of the controls. For desktop database forms, Access provides two default layouts. In the tabular layout, controls are arranged in columns and rows (something like a spreadsheet or a table). Labels are displayed in the form's Header section (similar to column headings). Access places the text box controls in the form's Detail section. In the stacked layout, controls appear in two columns, with labels in the column at the left and text box controls at the right. All the controls in the stacked layout are included in a single form section. Access uses the stacked layout for forms you create by using the Form command and for blank forms you create in Layout view.

By using the Move Up and Move Down commands in the Move group, you can reposition rows or a single cell in a layout. Another way to alter the arrangement of a layout is to merge or split cells. When you merge cells, one control spans two columns or rows. In contrast, when you split a cell in a layout, you can place two controls in that cell.

To move and position a control

→ Select the control, and then do either of the following:

- Drag the control to its new position.
- Use the arrow keys to reposition the control.

To move a control in Layout view

1. Open the form in Layout view and click the control you want to reposition.
2. On the **Arrange** tool tab, in the **Move** group, click **Move Up** or **Move Down**.

To merge two cells in Layout view

1. Open the form in Layout view and select the cells you want to merge.
2. On the **Arrange** tool tab, in the **Merge/Split** group, click **Merge**.

To split a cell in Layout view

1. Open the form in Layout view and select the cell you want to split.
2. On the **Arrange** tool tab, in the **Merge/Split** group, click **Split Vertically** or **Split Horizontally**.

To size and space controls in Design view

1. Open the form in Design view and select the control or controls you want to work with.

2. On the **Arrange** tool tab, in the **Sizing & Ordering** group, click **Size/Space**, and then click the option you want to apply to the controls.

To align controls in Design view

1. Open the form in Design view and then select the control or controls you want to work with.

2. On the **Arrange** tool tab, in the **Sizing & Ordering** group, click **Align**, and then click the option you want to apply to the controls.

To change the order of controls

1. Open the form in Design view and then select the control or controls you want to work with.

2. On the **Arrange** tool tab, in the **Sizing & Ordering** group, click **Send to Back** or **Bring to Front**.

Add and remove controls

In Design view and Layout view, the Controls group on the Design tool tab displays an icon for each type of control you can use on a form. A ScreenTip identifies the type of control.

Form controls are identified by a ScreenTip

> **See Also** For a description of each type of control and related control properties, see the next section, "Set control properties."

By default, Access enables the option Use Control Wizards and displays a wizard when you add a control such as a command button, combo box, list box, or chart.

The Command Button Wizard prompts you to select a category (such as Record Navigation) and an action (such as Go To First Record or Find Record). In the Form Operations category, the actions include Close Form, Print A Form, and Refresh Form Data, among others. You can display a text label on the button or select from a group of images that depict the button's function—such as a small form icon for a button set up to open a form.

In the Combo Box Wizard and List Box Wizard, you specify the source of the list items (a table, a query, or a list that you define). You also need to specify whether Access should remember the value selected in the list (which you might use in an expression) or save the value in a specific field.

Other controls for which Access provides a wizard are the option group, a chart control, and a subform.

When you add a hyperlink control or a web browser control to a form, Access opens the Insert Hyperlink dialog box. The dialog box provides similar options for each of these types of controls. For a hyperlink control, you can link to a file or a webpage, another database object, or an email address. You can also build a link for either type of control by providing a base URL (such as *http://bing.com*), an expression (such as */search?q=*), and a parameter. For example, you might name a parameter *Term* and give it the value *Microsoft + Office*, and the browser control would return search results related to Microsoft Office.

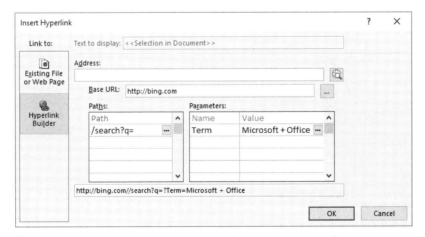

You can also use an expression to provide a value from a control on your form

If a label is associated with a control, when you delete the control, Access also deletes the label.

To add a control to a form

1. Open the form in Design view or Layout view.

2. On the **Design** tool tab, in the **Controls** group, click the icon for the type of control you want to add.

    Tip Point to controls to display their names in ScreenTips.

3. Click in the form where you want to place the control.

4. If Access displays a related control wizard, use the wizard to set up the control.

To remove a control from a form

→ Right-click the control, and then click **Delete**.

Set control properties

The properties for a form control are arranged on five tabs of the property sheet: Format, Data, Event, Other, and All. Form controls share some properties (such as the Name property), and each type of control also has specific properties related to its type. The following list describes some of the properties you often work with:

- The Format tab includes properties such as Caption, Height, Width, Text Align, and Visible. A control's Visible property shows or hides the control under conditions you define.

- The Data tab includes the Control Source property—the property that binds a control to data in a specific field or uses an expression to derive the control's data. Not all types of controls have a Control Source property. Bound controls (controls that are linked to a field) include text boxes, option groups (which contain option buttons or check boxes), combo boxes and list boxes, charts, and subforms and subreports. Unbound controls include labels, command and toggle buttons, tab controls, hyperlinks, the web browser control, lines, and images. The Data tab also includes properties such as Default Value, Validation Rule, and Validation Text.

    See Also For more information about field validation rules and the Default Value property, see "Objective 2.4: Create and modify fields."

- The Event tab lists properties such as On Click, Before Update, On Enter, and On Exit. You can associate a macro or a subprocedure written in Microsoft Visual Basic for Applications (VBA) with an event property to automate the operations of a form.

- The Other tab contains the Name property (in addition to other properties). You use the Name property to refer to a control in VBA code and in an expression. The Name property is not the same as the Caption property, which determines the display text associated with a control. Access creates a default value for the Name property (such as *Text10* or *List6*) when you add a control. You can update the Name property to make a control's purpose or relationship to a field clearer. You can use the ControlTip Text property on the Other tab to define the text for a ScreenTip that appears when you point to a control.

- The All tab displays all properties associated with a control.

Property sheet for a form control

The following list describes the purpose of each form control and identifies additional control properties related to the type of control:

- **Text box** Displays text fields and general number and currency fields. In addition to using the Width and Height properties to specify the size of a text box control, you can format a text box by setting properties such as Back Color, Border Style, Border Width, Font Name, and Font Size. For a field that uses the Long Text data type, set the Scroll Bars property to Vertical to more easily review the text that's displayed.

- **Label** Identifies fields and controls on the form. Formatting properties for labels include Font Name, Font Size, Font Weight and Border Style, Border Width, and Border Color. You can use the Special Effect property to give the label a sunken or raised look.

- **Button** Used to perform an action such as opening another form, navigating to records, or running macros or VBA code. You can set a variety of formatting properties for buttons. For example, you can add a picture to a button. You can use the Hover Color and Pressed Color properties to specify the color of the button and its text when you point to or press the button.

- **Tab** Provides a set of pages on which you can organize related data. In a database that tracks projects, for example, you could use one page of a tab control for schedule information, a second for budget fields, and a third for displaying data about task assignments. You can set properties for the tab control in general and for each page (tab). You can add text boxes, list boxes, buttons, and other types of controls to a page to define and interact with the data it displays.

- **Hyperlink** Links to a file, a webpage, or an email address. In a desktop database, you can also use a hyperlink to open another object in the database.

- **Web browser** Displays a file or a webpage on a form.

- **Navigation** Provides buttons that you can link to forms or reports.

> **See Also** For more information about using the navigation control, see "Objective 1.3: Navigate through a database."

- **Combo box** Lets users select an item from a list or specify a new item. You can restrict users from entering new items by setting the control's Limit To List property to Yes. You can format a combo box by setting font and border properties. A combo box's data properties include the Row Source property, which specifies the list's values, and Row Source Type, which indicates whether the list comes from fields in a table or a query or is defined by a value list that you create. Access provides a wizard that helps you set up a combo box.

- **List box** Displays a list of values from a table or a query or from a list that you define. As with a combo box, you use the Row Source and Row Source Type properties to set up the list.

- **Check box** Specifies yes/no or true/false choices. A check box has fewer formatting properties than other types of controls. Use the Control Source property to bind the control to a field.

- **Attachment** Is bound to a field defined with the Attachment data type. Use the entries on the Format tab of the property sheet to specify border styles, height, width, and any special effects.

4

- **Subform/subreport** Lets you embed another form or report within the form.

  See Also For more information about subforms, see "Create subforms" later in this topic.

- **Image** Displays a logo or another type of image on a form.

- **Option group** Creates an option group that can contain check boxes, option buttons, or toggle buttons. When you bind an option group to a field, the value of that field can be determined by which option button or check box a user selects in the group. For example, you could bind an option group to the field ShipOptions and include option buttons for Express, Second Day, and Ground.

- **Option button** Captures yes/no or true/false information. You can add a set of option button controls to an option group to set the value for the field bound to the option group.

- **Page break** Inserts a page break between pages of a multipage form.

- **Chart** Inserts a chart on a form. Access displays the Chart Wizard, which you use to select the fields whose data the chart displays, the type of chart, the chart's layout, and other properties.

- **Line** Adds a line to visually separate controls.

- **Toggle button** Captures yes/no information. When a toggle button is enabled (appears pressed in), its value is yes or true. When the button is not enabled, its value is false.

- **Rectangle** Adds a filled or empty rectangle to a form. You can enclose controls in a rectangle to help format the form.

- **Unbound object frame** Used for adding an object from another program to your form. The program needs to support object linking and embedding (OLE). You can add pictures, sounds, charts, slides, and worksheets, for example.

- **Bound object frame** Used for displaying and editing an OLE object field from the form's record source. You can display pictures and graphs on a form. For other types of objects, Access displays the icon representing the object's program.

By setting properties such as Back Color and Border Style in the property sheet, you can define or modify how a control appears. You can also set formatting properties for a control by working with commands on the Format tool tab when a form is open in Design view or Layout view. For example, in the Font group on the Format tool tab, you can make changes to font properties for labels and other controls on the form.

The alignment buttons in the Font group on the Format tool tab position the text in the label as flush left, flush right, or centered. In the Number group on the Format tool tab, you can apply a format to fields that use the Number, Currency, or Date/Time data type. For a date field, you can choose Medium Date, Long Date, Short Date, or another option from the Format list. The format you choose here affects how the date is displayed on the form, but it doesn't change the date format specified for the field in the table.

In the Control Formatting group on the Format tool tab, the Shape Fill command adds a background color to a control. You can use the Shape Outline command to modify the color and style of a control's borders. For a command button, you can use options on the Shape Effects menu to apply a shadow, a glow effect, or softened or beveled edges. Access enables the Change Shape command when you select a command button, tab control, or navigation button, for example. Use the options to display the button as an oval or another of the available shapes. For button controls, you can also apply a set of formats by choosing an option from the Quick Styles gallery.

To configure control properties

1. Open the form in Design view or Layout view, and open the form property sheet.

2. At the top of the property sheet, in the **Selection type** list, click the control you want to configure.

3. On the **Format**, **Data**, **Event**, **Other**, or **All** tab of the property sheet, specify the values for the control properties you want to set.

To format form controls

1. Open the form in Design view or Layout view, and select the control or controls you want to format.

2. Do one or more of the following:

   - In the **Font** group, choose a new font, font size, or font color; apply bold, italic, or underline formatting; add a background fill color; or align the text.

   - For **Number**, **Currency**, and **Date/Time** fields, use the options in the **Number** group to apply number, date/time, or currency formatting to the field.

3. In the **Control Formatting** group, do any of the following:

   - Use the **Quick Style** and **Change Shape** commands to format a button.

   - Use the **Shape Fill** command to add a background fill color to a control.

   - Use the **Shape Outline** command to apply line styles and colors to the control's borders.

   - Use the **Shape Effects** command to add a shadow or glow effect to a button control.

4

Modify data sources

A form and the controls that it contains are tied to a data source. For a form, a *data source*—also referred to as a *record source*—can be based on a single table, multiple tables, or a query (which is itself based on one or more tables). The data source for a specific control is governed by the Control Source property. The Control Source property can be set to a specific field in the form's record source or to an expression. For example, you can add a text box to a form and enter an expression such as *=Sum([ExtendedPrice])*[Discount]* to multiply the values in the ExtendedPrice field by the value of the Discount field to calculate the discounted amount of an order. You can modify the Control Source property for a specific control by choosing another field from the form's record source or by creating an expression for a calculated control.

You can choose a different table or query for the record source for a form or open the Query Builder, which is similar to the Query Designer. In the Query Builder, you can select other tables or queries to add to the form's record source and use the field list in the design grid to select the fields you want to include on the form. If a form is based on a query, the Query Builder displays the record source as a SQL statement that you can edit if you are familiar with SQL keywords and other elements.

See Also For more information about the Query Designer, see "Objective group 3: Create queries."

A form also has a Record Source Type property that you can set to one of three values to specify how users work with the form to insert and update data:

- **Dynaset** This is the default setting. When the Record Source Type property is set to Dynaset, you can edit bound controls based on a single table or on tables with a one-to-one relationship. For controls bound to fields based on tables with a one-to-many relationship, you cannot edit data from the linking field for the table on the "one" side of the relationship unless the Cascade Update option is set for the relationship between the tables.

- **Dynaset (Inconsistent Updates)** Specifying this setting makes all controls bound to a field editable.

- **Snapshot** Choosing this setting prevents updates to any of the fields displayed on a form.

See Also For more information about modifying data sources for forms and reports, see "Modify data sources" in "Objective 5.2: Configure report controls." For more information about the Expression Builder, see "Use calculated fields," in "Objective 3.3: Create calculated fields and grouping within queries."

To modify the data source of a form

1. Open the form in Design view, and open the form property sheet.

2. On the **Data** tab of the property sheet, click in the **Record Source** property box, and then do either of the following:

   - Select a different table or query from the list in the property box.

   - Click the ellipsis to open the Query Builder, use the Query Builder to modify the fields in the form's record source, and then close the Query Builder.

3. Set the **Record Source Type** property to **Dynaset**, **Dynaset (Inconsistent Updates)**, or **Snapshot**.

To modify the Control Source property

1. Open the form in Design view, and select the control you want to work with.

2. Open the form property sheet. On the **Data** tab of the property sheet, click in the **Control Source** property box, and then do either of the following:

   - Select a different field from the list in the property box.

   - Click the ellipsis to open the Expression Builder to create an expression for the control.

Manage labels

By default, Access includes a label when you add a control that can display data on a form. You can also use a label control for headings and to display descriptive or instructive text blocks on a form.

A label's Caption property is set by Access to match the Caption property set for a related field. You can change the text displayed in a label by selecting the label and editing the label's text. Access resizes the label to display the modified caption.

For a specific form, you can define the properties for a label control and then use those properties as default settings. (You can also set default control properties for other types of controls.)

Some properties you might set include Fore Color, Background Color, Border Style, and Border Color. You can then specify the label's formatting as the default formatting, and new labels you place on the form will use the default settings.

4

To update default settings for a label

1. Open the form in Design view or Layout view, and open the form property sheet.

2. Add a label control to the form, and then use options on the **Format** tool tab and on the **Format** tab of the property sheet to format the label as you want it to appear.

3. On the **Design** tool tab, in the **Controls** group, click **More**, and then click **Set Control Defaults**.

Create subforms

By creating a subform that you display within a main form, you can display data from related tables—for example, you can use a subform to display detailed budget records when the summary budget amount is displayed on the main form. You can define a main form and a subform when you use the Form Wizard. You can also use the SubForm Wizard to add a subform to a form you have already created. By default, Access displays the SubForm Wizard when you insert a subform/subreport control on a form.

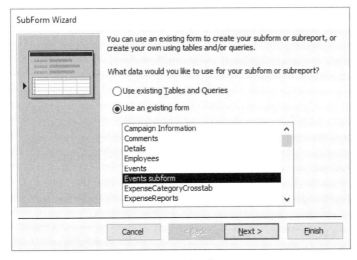

Base a subform on a table, query, or another form

You can base a subform on a table, query, or form you've already defined. When you base the subform on an existing table or query, the wizard displays a page on which you choose fields from one or more tables to include on the subform. You also define which field links the subform and the main form. If the table or query you selected has a relationship to the main form's record source, Access shows a list of fields you can choose from. If Access cannot determine the linking fields, it selects the Define My Own option on this page. You then need to select the linking fields you want to use.

If you want to fine-tune the work the wizard performed, select the subform control, and then on the property sheet, adjust the Height and Width properties or reposition the control by setting the Top and Left properties. You can also enter a message in the Status Bar Text property (on the Other tab of the property sheet) to describe the purpose of the subform.

To insert a subform control

1. Open the form in Design view.

2. On the **Design** tool tab, in the **Controls** group, click **Subform/Subreport**, and then click in the form where you want the subform to appear. Access displays the SubForm Wizard.

3. Follow the steps in the **SubForm Wizard** to select the form, table, or query on which to base the subform; select fields for the subform; and specify the field that links the subform and the main form.

4. Enter a name for the subform (or accept the default name that Access provides), and then click **Finish**.

4

Objective 4.2 practice tasks

The practice file for these tasks is located in the **MOSAccess2016\Objective4** practice file folder. The folder also contains a result file that you can use to check your work.

➤ Open the **Access_4-2** database.

➤ Open the Campaign Information form in Design view and do the following:

❑ Use the commands in the Sizing & Ordering group on the Arrange tool tab to align the labels to the left.

❑ Resize the text box controls so that they match the width of the narrowest control.

❑ Align the text boxes to the right.

❑ Use the *Spacing* options on the Size/Space menu to apply equal vertical space between the labels and the text boxes.

❑ Save and close the form.

➤ Open the Marketing Materials form in Layout view and do the following:

❑ Use the field list to add the Headline, Presentation, and Sales Kit fields to the form.

❑ Insert a new column to the right.

❑ Add a command button control to the top row of the new column.

❑ Configure the button to open the Task Details form and display all its records.

❑ Name the button MyButton1 and add the button caption Task details.

❑ Add a hyperlink control below the Task Details button.

❑ Configure the hyperlink to send a message to your email address. In the Text To Display field, enter Send reminder. In the Subject field, enter Marketing materials due.

❑ Change settings for the Record Source Type property to *Dynaset (Inconsistent)*.

❑ Save and close the Marketing Materials form.

➤ Open the Task Details form in Design view and do the following:

❑ Change the font of all the text box controls to *Arial*.

❑ Apply bold formatting to the Description field.

❑ In the property sheet, apply the *Medium Date* format to the Start Date and Due Date fields.

❑ Insert a subform in the area below the other controls. Base the subform on the existing Comments form. Use *TaskID* as the linking field. Name the subform <u>Comments</u>.

❑ Save and close the form.

➤ Open the **Access_4-2_results** database. Compare the databases to check your work. Then close the open databases.

Objective 4.3: Format forms

This topic describes some of the formatting features you can apply to a form. For example, it covers how to modify the tab order—the order in which you can move between controls by pressing the Tab key. It describes how to apply a theme to a form, how to insert images, and how to modify the background of a form. This topic also covers form properties related to sorting records in a form and printing a form.

Set tab order

Tab order determines the sequence in which controls gain focus as a user moves from field to field by pressing Tab. Carefully setting the tab order for a form can help users enter data in a logical manner (for example, first name, last name, and then middle initial instead of first name, street address, city, and then last name).

Access sets a default tab order as you add controls to a form, but this order might not be the most efficient. You can specify the tab order you want to use by working in the Tab Order dialog box or by setting the Tab Index and Tab Stop properties for a control in the control property sheet.

The Tab Order dialog box lists each section of the form and the fields and controls within that section. The fields are listed in the current tab order. The dialog box describes how to reorder the rows to set the tab order for the form. The Auto Order button creates a tab order that reflects the position of controls as they appear left to right and top to bottom on a form.

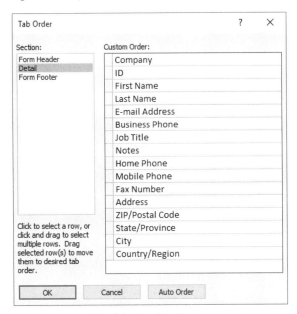

Drag a row to position it in the tab order

On the Other tab of the property sheet for a control, the Tab Index property specifies the order of controls, starting with 0 (zero) for the first control. You can exclude a control from the tab order by setting the control's Tab Stop property to No.

When you press Tab in the last control in the tab order, Access by default displays the next record in the form record source and then moves the focus to the first field in the tab order. You can use the Cycle property for a form to change this behavior. The Cycle property appears on the Other tab in the property sheet for the form. The All Records setting provides the default behavior. The Current Record option returns the focus to the first field in the tab order for the current record. The Current Page option (which applies to multipage forms) moves the focus to the first field in the tab order on the current page.

To set the tab order for a form

1. Open the form in Design view.
2. On the **Design** tool tab, in the **Tools** group, click **Tab Order**.
3. In the **Tab Order** dialog box, do either of the following, and then click **OK**:
   - Select the field or fields whose tab order you want to set, and then drag the field or fields to the tab position you want to use.
   - Click **Auto Order** to arrange the tab order to match the order of the form controls arranged left to right and top to bottom.

To set tab order properties for a control

1. Open the form in Design view and open the form property sheet.
2. At the top of the property sheet, in the **Selection type** list, select the control whose properties you want to set.
3. On the **Other** tab of the property sheet, set the **Tab Index** property to specify the tab position of this control. To exclude a control from the tab order, set the **Tab Stop** property to **No**.

To set the Cycle property for a form

1. On the **Design** tool tab, in the **Tools** group, click **Property Sheet**.
2. At the top of the property sheet, in the **Selection type** list, select **Form**.
3. On the **Other** tab of the property sheet, set the **Cycle** property to **All Records**, **Current Record**, or **Current Page**.

4

Configure print settings

If you create a form that you expect to print, you should consider the setting for the Layout For Print property. Setting this property to Yes or No determines whether Access uses screen fonts or printer fonts. Screen fonts are installed on your computer for on-screen display. They usually display text at a lower resolution than printer fonts. Printer fonts are designed to more accurately represent the characters in a font. (When you set up a printer, the printer might install additional screen fonts. The fonts available are those installed as part of your printer's setup and depend on your printer.)

The appearance of characters and symbols displayed with a screen font can differ some-what when they are printed. For example, you might design a form on a system that uses a printer different from the one you use to print the form. When you print the form, Access displays a message indicating that the form was designed for another type of printer. If you proceed to print the form, your printer might substitute different fonts.

The Layout For Print property appears near the bottom of the Format tab on the form property sheet. (Be sure to select Form from the Selection Type list to display the correct list of properties.)

The default setting for the property is No, which specifies that printer fonts installed on your computer will not be available for any font settings. Screen fonts and TrueType fonts are available. Specifying Yes makes screen fonts unavailable; printer fonts and TrueType fonts are available. (TrueType fonts are printer fonts that appear accurately on the screen and on many inkjet printers. TrueType fonts do not display as well on other printing platforms, such as certain PostScript printers.)

See Also For more information about printing from Access databases, see "Objective 1.5: Print and export data."

To set the Layout For Print property

1. Open the form in Design view or Layout view, and open the form property sheet.

2. On the property sheet, in the **Selection type** list, click **Form**.

3. On the **Format** tab of the property sheet, click in the **Layout for Print** box, and then select the setting you want to apply to the form.

Sort records

When you base a form on a table or a query, the form inherits any sort order defined for its record source. You can change the sort order for the records in a form without changing the sort order specified in its record source. To do this, you use the Order By and Order By On Load properties.

These properties appear on the Data tab in a form property sheet. In the Order By property, you can enter the name of the field (enclosed in brackets) by which you want to sort the records. You can use more than one field by separating field names with a comma. By default, records are sorted in ascending order. Enter *DESC* after a field's names to sort in descending order.

The setting you specify for the Order By property is saved with the form, but the sort order is not automatically applied when you open the form unless you set Order By On Load to Yes.

Tip When you have a form open in Datasheet view, you can sort records by selecting a field and then clicking the appropriate Sort button in the Sort & Filter group on the Home tab.

To set the Order By and Order By On Load properties

1. Open the form in Design view or Layout view, and open the form property sheet.

2. On the property sheet, in the **Selection type** list, click **Form**.

3. On the **Data** tab of the property sheet, click in the **Order By** box, and then enter the name of the field or fields you want to sort by, enclosing the field names in brackets and separating field names by using a comma.

4. To sort a field in descending order, enter <u>DESC</u> after the field's name.

5. To sort the records when the form is opened, set **Order By On Load** to **Yes**.

Apply themes to forms

Themes are used throughout Microsoft Office to provide a common look to documents, spreadsheets, presentations, and database objects. In Access, themes control colors and fonts. For forms, themes affect the color and font used in the form's header and the font used in labels and text box controls.

4

You apply a theme to a form by using the Themes gallery. When the Live Preview feature is enabled, a preview of a theme is displayed when you point to an option in the gallery.

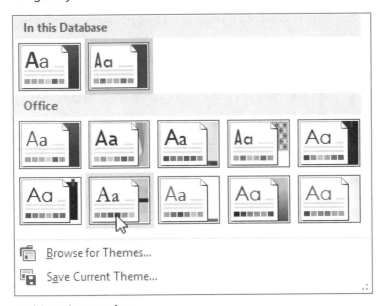

Applying a theme to a form

Tip If Live Preview is not enabled, click Options on the File tab. On the General page of the Access Options dialog box, select Enable Live Preview.

By default, the Themes gallery is divided into two groups. The In This Database group shows the default database theme and any other theme applied to a database object. The Office group lists the themes that Access provides. You can browse to locate other theme files (which use the .thmx file name extension). These themes might be available on your network or in a different folder on your local computer.

When you apply a theme to a form, that theme is inherited by other objects in the database by default. Applying a theme to all the objects in your database in a single step saves time, but you can also apply a theme to a single object or change the theme for a set of objects that share a theme. The Themes gallery provides the following options:

- Apply Theme To All Matching Objects
- Apply Theme To This Object Only
- Make This Theme The Database Default

When you apply a theme to a specific object, Access lists this theme in the In This Database group in the Themes gallery. A ScreenTip identifies which object the theme applies to or whether the theme applies to the database.

You aren't bound by the formatting in a theme. You can apply a different color scheme to a form, for example, and then update objects that use the same theme. You can also modify the font used in a form. If you specify a different color scheme or font for a form, you can save those settings as a new theme. The themes you define and save are displayed in the Themes gallery in their own group, named *Custom*.

To apply a theme to a form

1. Open the form in Design view or Layout view.
2. On the **Design** tool tab, in the **Themes** group, click **Themes**.
3. Right-click the thumbnail for the theme you want to apply, and then click **Apply Theme to This Object Only**.

To modify the color scheme for a theme

1. Open the form in Design view or Layout view.
2. On the **Design** tool tab, in the **Themes** group, click **Colors**, and then select the color scheme you want to use.

To define a custom color scheme

1. On the **Design** tool tab, in the **Themes** group, click **Colors**, and then click **Customize Colors**.
2. In the **Create New Theme Colors** dialog box, specify the colors for the theme elements (such as **Text/Background—Dark 1**).

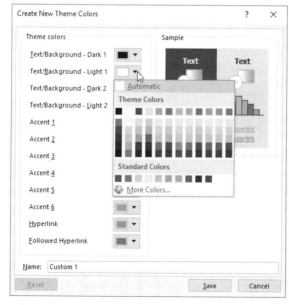

Select colors for specific elements

3. Enter a name for the custom color scheme, and then click **Save**.

To modify the font scheme for a theme

1. Open the form in Design view or Layout view.

2. On the **Design** tool tab, in the **Themes** group, click **Fonts**, and then click the font scheme you want to use.

To define a custom font scheme

1. On the **Design** tool tab, in the **Themes** group, click **Fonts**, and then click **Customize Fonts**.

2. In the **Create New Theme Fonts** dialog box, specify the heading font and body font.

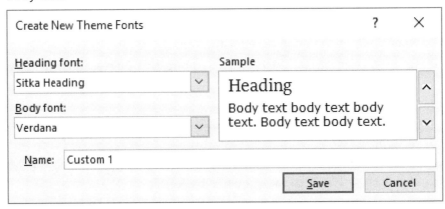

Select a font for headings and body text

3. Enter a name for the custom font scheme, and then click **Save**.

Control form positioning

When a form is open in Layout view, you can use options in the Position group on the Arrange tool tab to adjust the spacing between controls, the margins around the text displayed by a control, and how controls are anchored within the layout.

Each setting on the Control Margins menu—None, Narrow, Medium, and Wide— progressively increases the space between the upper-left corner of a control and the position of the control text. The Wide setting can obscure text in a text box that is less than approximately 0.3 inches in height (assuming the font size you are using is the default 11 points).

Settings in the Control Padding area (also None, Narrow, Medium, and Wide) affect the space between controls in the layout.

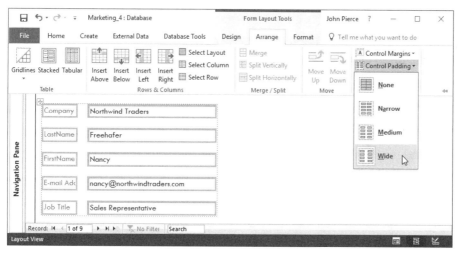

Adjust padding to space controls on a form

Resizing a form window can affect how controls are arranged. By applying one of the anchoring options that Access provides, you can fasten controls to the top left (the default position), top right, bottom left, or one of the other anchoring positions. After you select an anchoring option, resize the form window to test the effect. You can anchor the entire layout or specific elements on a form. For example, if you add a line to set off a section of a form, apply the Stretch Across Top anchoring option to have the line stretch across the top of the form when the form window is resized.

To specify margins for text boxes on a form

1. On the **Arrange** tool tab, in the **Rows & Columns** group, click **Select Layout**.
2. In the **Position** group, click **Control Margins**, and then click the option you want to apply.

To insert padding between controls on a form

1. On the **Arrange** tool tab, in the **Rows & Columns** group, click **Select Layout**.
2. In the **Position** group, click **Control Padding**, and then click the option you want to apply.

To apply an anchoring option to a form

1. On the **Arrange** tool tab, in the **Rows & Columns** group, click **Select Layout**.
2. In the **Position** group, click **Anchoring**, and then choose the option you want to apply.

Modify the background of a form

You can insert an image as the background for a form. After you add the image, you can set the following properties to control the display of the image (the settings in one or more of these properties affect the options for others):

- **Picture Type** Use the Embedded option if you want Access to add a copy of the image to the form. With this option, you know the image is available whenever you load the form, but adding a copy of the image increases the size of the form and the database. If you choose Link, Access uses the path and file name specified in the Picture property to locate the image file each time you open the form. If the file is moved, Access displays it only after you update the path. If you use the Shared option, Access adds a copy of the image to a system table. You can then select the image from the Picture property list to display it as a background in other database objects.

- **Picture** This property specifies the image file used as the background. You can choose an image from the list or click the ellipsis if you want to select a different image file.

- **Picture Tiling** If you set the Picture Size Mode property to Clip or Zoom and the image you insert is smaller than the form's dimensions, set this property to Yes to display multiple copies of the image on the form.

- **Picture Alignment** When the Picture Size Mode property is set to Clip or Zoom, you can choose an option in the Picture Alignment property to center the image or place it in a corner of the form.

- **Picture Size Mode** This property controls the size at which Access displays the image. The options include the following:

  - **Clip** Access trims the borders of the image so that it fits the size of the form.

  - **Zoom** Access increases or decreases the size of the image to fit the size of the form. With this option, Access retains the proportions of the image.

  - **Stretch, Stretch Horizontal, Stretch Vertical** When you choose one of these options, Access resizes the image to fit the size of the form, but the image's proportions can be distorted.

For a form that you work with in Datasheet view, you can apply a color you specify (a theme color, a standard color, or a color you define) to alternating rows in the datasheet. (Access displays a form in Datasheet view when you select Datasheet in the Default View property for the form or you select Datasheet as the layout option when you use the Form Wizard.)

To add an image to a form's background

1. Open the form in Design view or Layout view.

2. On the **Format** tool tab, in the **Background** group, click **Background Image**, and then do either of the following:

   - Select an image in the **Image** gallery.

   - Click **Browse** to locate the image file you want to use. Select the image file in the **Insert Picture** dialog box, and then click **OK**.

To set properties for a background image

1. Open the form in Design view or Layout view, and open the form property sheet.

2. In the property sheet, in the **Selection type** list, click **Form**.

3. On the **Format** tab of the property sheet, set the values you want to use for the following properties: **Picture Type**, **Picture**, **Picture Tiling**, **Picture Alignment**, and **Picture Size Mode**.

To apply an alternating row color

1. Open the form in Datasheet view.

2. On the **Datasheet** tool tab, in the **Formatting** group, click **Alternate Row Color**, and then click the color you want to apply.

4

Insert form headers and footers

As described in "Objective 4.1: Create forms," a form includes three sections: Detail, Header, and Footer. When you first create a form in Design view or Layout view, Access displays only the Detail section. You can use options in the Header/Footer group on the Design tool tab to insert a logo, a title, and the date and time (in various formats) in your form. The options add the form element to the form's Header section, but you can drag it to the footer section to include it there.

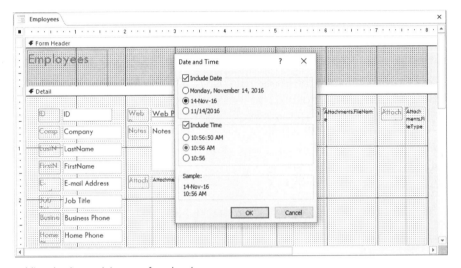

Adding the date and time to a form header

Tip You can display or hide the Header and Footer sections in Design view by right-clicking in the Detail section of the form and then clicking Form Header/Footer.

The commands in the Header/Footer group insert built-in elements, but you can add other controls to a form's header or footer. For example, you can add button controls to the header or footer section to save room for text boxes and other controls in the Detail section.

See Also For more information about adding form controls, see "Add and remove controls," in "Objective 4.2: Configure form controls."

To insert information in a form header or footer

1. Open the form in Design view or Layout view.

2. On the **Design** tool tab, in the **Header/Footer** group, do any of the following:

   - To add a logo to the form header, click **Logo**. In the **Insert Picture** dialog box, navigate to and select the logo image file, and then click **Open**.

   - To add a title to the form header, click **Title**. In the **Auto_Header()** control that appears, replace the default title with the title you want.

   - To add the date or time to the form header, click **Date and Time**. In the **Date and Time** dialog box, select the check boxes for the elements you want to include, select the element formats you want, and then click **OK**.

Insert images

Forms can display logos or images related to the purpose of the database—product thumbnails, project locations, or employee portraits, for example.

As you do with form backgrounds, you should update settings for the following properties that affect the appearance and behavior of the image: Picture Type, Picture, Picture Tiling, Picture Alignment, and Picture Size Mode.

See Also For more information about how to use these properties, see "Modify the background of a form" earlier in this topic.

To insert an image on a form

1. Open the form in Design view or Layout view.

2. On the **Design** tool tab, in the **Controls** group, click **Insert Image**, and then click **Browse** to open the Insert Picture dialog box.

3. In the **Insert Picture** dialog box, select the image file, and then click **OK**.

4. Open the form property sheet. At the top of the property sheet, in the **Selection Type** list, click **Form**.

5. On the **Format** tab of the property sheet, set the values you want to use for the following properties: **Picture Type**, **Picture**, **Picture Tiling**, **Picture Alignment**, and **Picture Size Mode**.

4

Objective 4.3 practice tasks

The practice files for these tasks are located in the **MOSAccess2016\ Objective4** practice file folder. The folder also contains a result file that you can use to check your work.

➤ Open the **Access_4-3** database and do the following:

☐ Open the Events form in Layout view.

☐ Apply the *Organic* theme to this form only.

☐ Apply the *Blue Warm* color scheme to the form.

☐ Apply the *Corbel* font set to the form.

☐ Save the form, and then save the modified theme as a custom theme named <u>MyAccessTheme</u>.

☐ Add the **Access_4-3a** image to the Events form as a tiled background image.

☐ Save and close the form.

➤ Open the Campaign Information form in Design view and do the following:

☐ Modify the form's tab order so that it follows this sequence: Country, Language, Launch Date, End Date, and Campaign Budget.

☐ Open the property sheet and exclude the Campaign ID, Last Name, Presentation, and Events controls from the tab order.

☐ Sort the records in the Campaign Information form in descending order by country/region.

☐ Add the date and time to the Header section of the Campaign Information form. Select the formats *MM/DD/YYYY* and *HH:MM*. Save and close the form.

➤ Open the **Access_4-3_results** database. Compare the databases to check your work, and then close the databases.

Objective group 5

Create reports

The skills tested in this section of the Microsoft Office Specialist exam for Microsoft Access 2016 relate to creating and modifying reports. Specifically, the following objectives are associated with this set of skills:

5.1 Create reports

5.2 Configure report controls

5.3 Format reports

You can use reports to create a filtered view of your data, to group and summarize data, and to provide data in a format that's suitable for sharing, printing, and presentations. You format reports and report elements by adding, grouping, and sorting fields; modifying data sources; and adding controls and labels. After you format your report, you can preview it in print preview to see how the report's printed pages will look—for example, whether the margins are set correctly, whether formatting is in place, and whether the information you want in the report's header and footer sections is included.

This chapter guides you in studying ways of creating and formatting reports and configuring report controls.

To complete the practice tasks in this chapter, you need the practice files contained in the **MOSAccess2016\Objective5** practice file folder. For more information, see "Download the practice files" in this book's introduction.

5

Objective 5.1: Create reports

The Report command creates a basic report that includes all the fields in the table or query you select in the Navigation Pane. The Report Wizard leads you through options for how to group, sort, and summarize the records in a report and provides a choice of layouts. If you want to create a report from scratch, you can create a blank report that opens in Layout view or in Design view. As with forms, Layout view shows data from the report's record source as you add fields and controls to the report. You cannot update the data in the report window, but you can open a table while working on a report if you need to update its data. In Design view, you don't see data, but Design view offers more flexibility in how you can arrange the fields in a report. The Labels command displays a wizard that creates labels for an address list (similar to the mail-merge operation in Microsoft Word.) You provide information such as label size, font attributes, and the data fields to include on the labels.

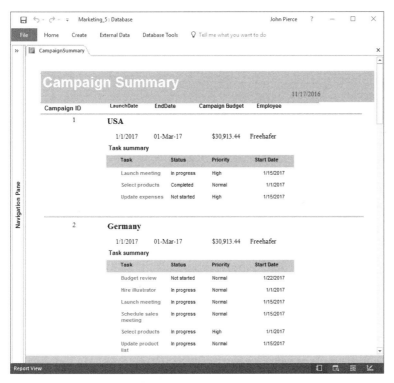

A completed report open in Report view

Use the Report Wizard

Run the Report Wizard when you want help creating a report that includes fields from more than one table or query. After you select the fields for the report, the wizard prompts you to specify the first grouping level for the report. For example, you can choose By Suppliers or By Products for a report that includes fields from both of these tables. The wizard displays a preview that shows how the report's records will be organized. Base your decision on the view of the data you want the report to provide.

In this example, the report can display which products each supplier provides or all suppliers for individual products.

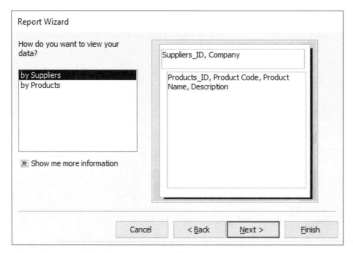

Grouping records in the Report Wizard

You can select additional fields to use as grouping levels by opening the Grouping Intervals dialog box. Grouping intervals depend on a field's data type. For a Date/Time field, you can use an interval such as *year* or *quarter*. For a numeric field, you can specify an incremental value such as *1,000*. You can group text fields by a specific number of characters—for example, the first three letters in company or product names.

In the wizard, you can specify as many as four fields by which to sort data. You can use only those fields not specified for a grouping level. You can also apply a function such as Sum or Avg to summarize report data, and you can choose between showing only summary data or both detail records (for example, itemized expenses in a specific budget category) and summary data (the total for that category).

For the report layout, you can choose Stepped, Block, or Outline. A preview shows how each option affects the layout. You can specify page orientation and whether the wizard should adjust the width of each field so that fields fit on the page. Selecting the option to adjust field width might cause some text boxes to display only a portion of the field's data.

> **See Also** For more information about moving and sizing controls, see "Move controls" in "Objective 4.2: Configure form controls."

To create a report with the Report Wizard

1. On the **Create** tab, in the **Reports** group, click **Report Wizard**.
2. On the first page of the **Report Wizard**, expand the **Tables/Queries** list and select the first table or query you want to use for this report.

3. In the **Available Fields** list, do either of the following:

- Select the field or fields you want to include in the query, and then click the arrow button (>) to move the fields to the **Selected Fields** list.

- Click the chevron button (>>) to move all the fields to the **Selected Fields** list.

4. Repeat steps 2 and 3 to include other tables or queries in the report and add the fields you want to include. Then click **Next**.

5. On the second page of the **Report Wizard**, specify the field or fields by which you want to group records in the report.

6. If you add a grouping level that includes dates, numeric values, or text fields, click **Grouping Options**, select the intervals by which to group those values, and then click **OK**.

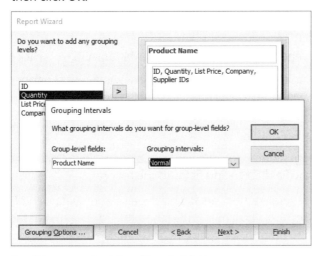

Specifying a grouping interval for a text field

7. Click **Next**.

8. Choose up to four fields to establish the record sort order. If you want to sort a field in descending order, click the **Ascending** button adjacent to the field to change the sort order.

9. If the report fields include numeric values, click **Summary Options** and then in the **Summary Options** dialog box, do the following:

   a. Select the check box for each summary function you want to apply to each of the fields.

5

    b. Choose an option to view only summary data or both detail and summary data.

    c. Click **OK**.

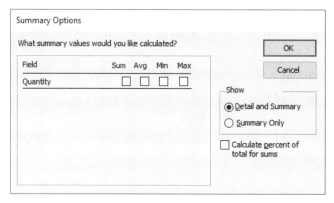

Summary functions include Sum, Avg, Min, and Max

10. Click **Next**. Choose a report layout and a page orientation, and then click **Next**.

11. Enter a name for the report, choose whether to preview the report or open the report in Design view, and then click **Finish**.

Create reports from scratch

When you create reports from scratch, you can work in Design view or Layout view. In either view, you work with the field list to add fields to the report.

Like forms, reports contain several sections, including Page Header, Detail, and Page Footer. In the Page Header section, you can include labels that identify the data fields that are included in the Detail section, for example. You can use the Page Footer section to display page numbers and similar information. A report can also include the Report Header and Report Footer sections. The Report Header section appears only on the first page of a report and can be used to display a title or a logo. The Report Footer section appears at the end of the report. You can use this section to display a grand total of values on the report.

In Layout view, a report's controls are contained within a layout that helps manage the alignment and arrangement of controls. Access provides two default layouts: tabular and stacked. In the tabular layout, controls are arranged in columns and rows. Labels are displayed in the Page Header section of the report. Text box controls that display field data are included in the Detail section of the report. In the stacked layout, controls appear in two columns, with labels in the left column and field controls in the right column. All controls in the stacked layout are included in a report's Detail section.

By default, Access uses the tabular layout for reports you first open in Layout view. When you add the first field, Access displays a button (identified by a lightning bolt icon) beside the field. You can use this button to switch the report from the tabular layout to the stacked layout.

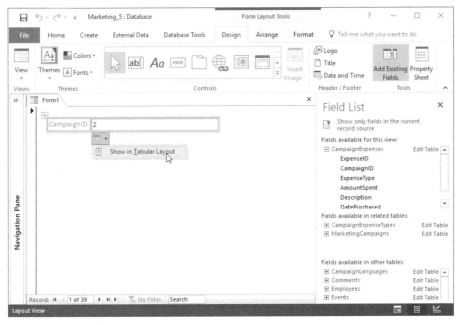

Drag fields from the field list to the report window; switch the layout if you need to

The Report Design command opens a blank report page in Design view. The page shows three of the sections you can use in a report—Page Header, Detail, and Page Footer. The grid marks and the ruler help you align and position fields. Access highlights the ruler when you drag a control to indicate the control's relative position. By right-clicking a control, you can work with the Align, Size, and Position commands to adjust the placement and dimensions of the control.

5

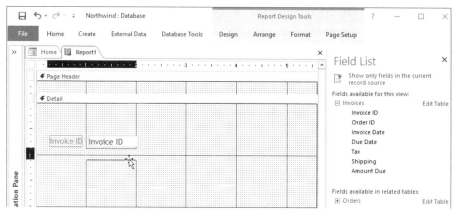

Check the ruler when you drag a control

You locate most of a report's controls in its Detail section, including labels and text boxes related to the report's data. You can also use the commands in the Header/ Footer group on the Design tool tab to add information to the Report Header and Report Footer sections by inserting an element such as a title, a logo, a date, and page numbers.

See Also For more information about adding elements to headers or footers, see "Add information to report headers and footers" in "Objective 5.3: Format reports."

When you work in Design view or in Layout view, you can add controls to a report to supplement the controls Access creates when you insert fields. For example, you might include additional labels, an image, or a subreport control that displays data from a related table or query.

See Also For more information about working with controls and setting control properties, see "Objective 4.2: Configure form controls"; "Add controls to a report" in "Objective 5.2: Configure report controls"; and "Format report elements" in "Objective 5.3: Format reports."

When you have a report open in Design view, the Arrange tool tab includes the Sizing & Ordering group. This group provides commands you can apply to controls to modify their size, the spacing between them, and their alignment.

Part of creating a report is to specify report properties. In the report property sheet, you can set properties for each report section, for controls, and for the report itself. For example, set the Default View property for the report to Report View or print pre-view depending on how you want Access to display the report when you open it.

To modify reports already included in a database, open the report in Design view or Layout view to make changes to the report's fields, properties, and formatting.

To create a report from scratch

1. On the **Create** tab, in the **Reports** group, do one of the following:

   - Click **Blank Report** to open the new report in Layout view.
   - Click **Report Design** to open the new report in Design view.

2. In the field list, click **Show All Tables** (if no tables are shown), and then click the plus sign (+) beside the table you want to use as the report's record source.

3. From the field list, drag the fields you want to include on the report and place them in the report window. You can align and reposition fields after you place them.

4. On the **Design** tool tab, click **Property Sheet**.

5. In the property sheet, specify properties for the report and the report controls.

To save a report

→ On the **Quick Access Toolbar**, click **Save**, and then enter a name for the report.

To open a report in Design view

→ In the **Navigation Pane**, right-click the report, and then click **Design View**.

To open a report in Layout view

→ In the **Navigation Pane**, right-click the report, and then click **Layout View**.

To open the report property sheet

1. Open the form in Design view or Layout view.

2. On the **Design** tool tab, in the **Tools** group. click **Property Sheet**.

To display the report field list

→ On the **Design** tool tab, in the **Tools** group. click **Add Existing Fields**.

To arrange controls in Design view

1. In the report, select the control or controls you want to work with.

2. On the **Arrange** tool tab, in the **Sizing & Ordering** group, do the following to adjust the report's design:

   - To adjust the size and spacing between selected controls, click **Size/Space**, and then click the option you want to apply to the controls.
   - To align selected controls, click **Align**, and then click the option you want to apply to the controls.
   - To change the position of a control or selected controls, click **Send to Back** or **Bring to Front**.

5

Objective 5.1 practice tasks

The practice file for these tasks is located in the **MOSAccess2016\Objective5** practice file folder. The folder also contains a result file that you can use to check your work.

➤ Open the **Access_5-1** database and do the following:

- ❏ If the Info Bar opens below the ribbon, click the *Enable Content* button.
- ❏ Use the Report command to create a report based on the ExpenseSummary query.
- ❏ Close the report, and save it with the name <u>MyExpenseSummary</u>.

➤ Use the Report Wizard to create the following report:

- ❏ Use the MarketingCampaigns table and the ExpenseReport query.
- ❏ From the MarketingCampaigns table, add all fields other than EndDate and Employee ID.
- ❏ From the ExpenseReport query, add the ExpenseType and AmountSpent fields.
- ❏ Group the report by ExpenseType. Keep the group option set to *Normal*.
- ❏ Sort the report by country/region.
- ❏ In the Summary Options dialog box, select *Avg* for CampaignBudget and *Sum* for the AmountSpent field. Keep the Show option set to *Detail* and *Summary*.
- ❏ Use a landscape orientation and the Block format layout.
- ❏ Keep the option to adjust field widths selected.
- ❏ Name the report <u>MyExpenseReport</u>, and keep the option to preview the report.

➤ Use the Report Design command to create a blank report named <u>MyReport</u>.

➤ Open the **Access_5-1_results** database. Compare the two databases to check your work. Then close the open databases.

Objective 5.2: Configure report controls

This topic describes how to work with fields and controls in a report. It explains how to group and sort records, add controls, manage a report's data source, and work with labels.

Group and sort records

Specifying how records are grouped in a report is an important aspect of the report's design. You can set grouping levels when you use the Report Wizard and by using the Group & Sort command when you work with a report in Design view or Layout view.

When you group records in Design view or Layout view, you work in the Group, Sort, And Total pane at the bottom of the report window. You can add one or more group header sections to the report based on the fields the report contains. If you work in Layout view, Access displays more clearly how the selections you make in the Group, Sort, And Total pane affect the report's organization. Access doesn't show this level of detail in Design view.

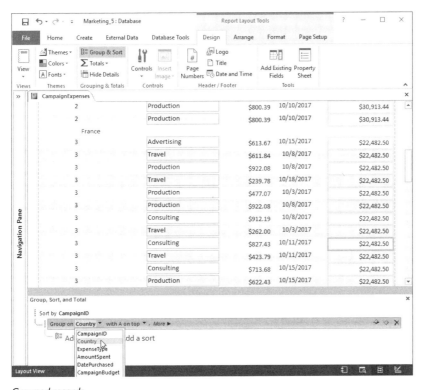

Grouped records

You can sort records within each grouping level. For example, in a budget report, you could group records first by country or region and then sort records within that group by expense category. You could also group by expense category and sort records within that group by the date of the expense.

The More arrow in the Group, Sort, And Total pane displays additional options that you can set for grouping and sorting fields.

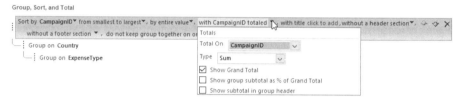

Additional options for grouping, sorting, and summarizing records

The following list describes the options as Access displays them, left to right:

- **Sort order** Use this option to specify the sort order, either ascending or descending.

- **Group interval** Use this option to specify how records are grouped. You can group a text field on the first letter, for example, which would group all items that start with A together, all items that start with B, and so on. Date fields can be grouped by day, week, month, quarter, or an interval you define.

- **Totals** You can add totals for multiple fields and apply different summary functions (Sum and Avg or Min and Max, for example) to the same field.

- **Title** Use this option to change the title of the field being summarized. The title is used for the column heading and for labeling summary fields in headers and footers.

- **With/Without a header section** Use this setting to add or remove the header section for each group. Access moves the grouping field to the header when you add the header section. Access prompts you to remove any controls (other than the grouping field) from the header when you remove it.

- **With/Without a footer section** Use this setting to add or remove the footer section that follows each group. When you remove a footer section that contains controls, Access asks for confirmation to delete the controls.

- **Keep group together** The settings for this option determine how groups are laid out on the page when the report is printed.

The options available for summarizing field values depend on the data type of the field you select. For numeric fields, the range of options include Sum, Avg, Count, Max, and Min. For text and Date/Time fields, the Count options are available—either Count Values or Count Records. For a summary report, you can use the Hide Details option in the Grouping & Totals group to show only the summary fields.

> **See Also** As you can for forms, you can use the Order By and Order By On Load properties to change the sort order for the records in a report without changing the sort order specified in its record source. For more information, see "Sort records" in "Objective 4.3: Format forms."

To group and sort records in a report

1. Open the report in Design view or Layout view.
2. On the **Design** tool tab, in the **Grouping & Totals** group, click **Group & Sort**.
3. In the **Group, Sort, and Total** pane, do the following:
   a. Click **Add a group**, and then select the field to group by.
   b. Click **More**, and then specify settings for sorting, grouping intervals, totals, title, header and footer sections, and how to keep groups together on the page.

To summarize values on a report

1. Open the report in Design view or Layout view.
2. In the report, select the field you want to summarize.
3. On the **Design** tool tab, in the **Grouping & Totals** group, click **Totals**, and then choose the summary function you want to apply.

Modify data sources

A report is tied to the data in a single table, multiple tables, or a query (which is itself based on one or more tables). Many report controls are bound to specific fields in the report's data source, which is also called its *record source*. When you create a report, Access builds the record source depending on tables and fields you select. You can also specify the record source yourself when you work in Design view or Layout view.

The data source for a specific control is governed by its Control Source property. The Control Source property can be set to a specific field in the report's record source or to an expression. For example, you can add a text box to a report and then enter an expression such as =[City] & ", " & " " & [State/Province] & " " & [Postal Code] to create the last line of an address block. In the property sheet, you can modify the Control Source property for a specific control by selecting another field or by using an expression you enter or one that you create by using the Expression Builder.

> **See Also** For more information about the Expression Builder, see "Objective 3.3: Create calculated fields and grouping within queries."

5

You can base a report (or multiple reports) on a query that you've designed and saved as an object in your database. However, if you modify the query, you might also affect the design of the report. To work around this possibility, you can embed a query in the report's Record Source property. An embedded query is not saved as a separate object, so any changes you make to the embedded query are also reflected in the report. Access creates an embedded query when you build a report in Design view or Layout view by adding fields from the field list. The Report Wizard creates an embedded query when you select fields from more than one table.

To modify the record source for a report, you can choose a different table or query or open the Query Builder. Use the Query Builder to add or remove fields for the current record source or to create the record source yourself.

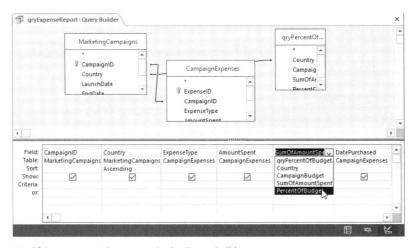

Modifying a report's data source in the Query Builder

See Also For information about working in the query design grid, see "Objective group 3: Create queries."

When you open the Query Builder in a report that is based on a single table, Access might prompt you to create a query based on the table, which converts the report's record source to an embedded query. After updating the record source, test the query by running it, which opens the query in Datasheet view.

Tip You can save an embedded query as an object in your database by clicking Save As in the Close group on the Design tool tab in the Query Builder.

To modify a report's record source

1. Open the report in Design view or Layout view, and open the property sheet.

2. On the **Data** tab of the property sheet, in the **Selection type** list, click **Report**.

3. Click in the **Record Source** box, and then do either of the following:

   - Select a different table or query from the list in the property box.

   - Click the ellipsis to open the Query Builder, use the Query Builder to modify the fields in the report's record source, and then close the Query Builder. If prompted, click **Yes** in the message box to confirm that you want to modify the Record Source property.

To modify the Control Source property for the selected control

1. Open the report in Design view or Layout view, and open the property sheet.

2. On the **Data** tab of the property sheet, click in the **Control Source** box, and then do either of the following:

   - Select a different field from the list.

   - Click the ellipsis to open the Expression Builder, and then create an expression for the control.

Add controls to a report

Reports are designed primarily to present and share data (unlike forms or tables, which you use to enter, update, and delete data). For a report, you often work only with label and text box controls to identify and present data. For example, you might add a label to identify a summary field in a group header section or to provide a title in the Report Header section. You can add a text box to a report and then write an expression to create a calculated field. You can add an image control to enhance the appearance of a report. When you are adding controls in Layout view, you can expand the area of a layout by inserting rows or columns.

See Also For more information about how to work with specific controls, including how to use the control wizards, see "Objective 4.2: Configure form controls."

Although the data is more static in a report than in a form or a table, you can use a command button to perform an action related to the report or add a hyperlink control to display a website or an email address. In Report view, command buttons and hyperlinks are operational. In print preview, Access doesn't display a command button, and a hyperlink appears as static text.

You can insert a subreport into a main report to provide related information. You can create the subreport by using the Report Wizard or by using the Subreport Wizard. In either case, the subreport must contain a field you can use to link it to the main report.

The Subreport Wizard appears when you add a subreport control to the report page.

5

In the wizard, you can select a report you want to use as the subreport or select an option to base the subreport on an existing table or query.

To add controls to a report

1. Open the report in Design view or Layout view.

2. On the **Design** tool tab, click **Controls**. In the **Controls** gallery, click the type of control you want to add, and then click in the report page where you want to add the control.

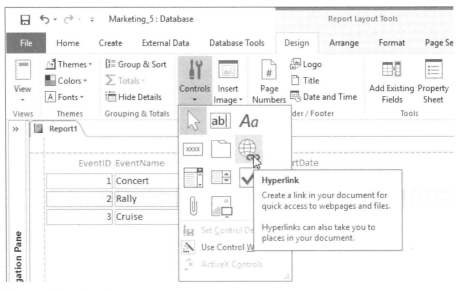

The report Controls gallery

3. If prompted, work with the control wizard for the type of control you are adding.

To insert a subreport control

1. Open the main report in Design view or Layout view.

2. On the **Design** tool tab, click **Controls**. In the **Controls** gallery, select the **Subform/Subreport** control, and then click in the main report where you want to place the subreport.

3. Follow the steps in the **Subreport Wizard** to select the report, table, or query on which to base the subreport, select fields for the subreport, and specify the field that links the subreport and the main report.

To work with control layouts in Layout view

1. On the **Arrange** tool tab, in the **Table** group, do either of the following:

    - To apply a different layout to the report, select all the fields in the report, and then click **Stacked** or **Tabular**.

    - To insert a row in the layout, click a cell in the adjacent row. In the **Rows & Columns** group, click **Select Row**, and then click **Insert Above** or **Insert Below**.

    - To insert a column in the layout, click a cell in the adjacent column. In the **Rows & Columns** group, click **Select Column**, and then click **Insert Left** or **Insert Right**.

Add and modify labels

When you add a text, number, or date field to a report, Access creates a text box to display the field's data and creates an associated label to display the field's name or caption. (Access also creates an associated label for other types of fields, including lookup fields and fields that use the AutoNumber data type.) You can then use the techniques described elsewhere in this chapter to format, size, and position the labels to fit the report's design.

See Also For more information, see "Add controls to a report" earlier in this topic and "Format report elements" in "Objective 5.3: Format reports."

To work with the full range of properties available for a label control, open the property sheet. Specify values on the Format tab of the property sheet for properties such as Width, Height, Back Style, Special Effect, and Font Size. On the Other tab of the property sheet, you can replace the default label name.

You can also add labels to a report (or a form) that aren't associated with fields. You might use a freestanding label to provide instructional text or to display a heading in a report.

When you add a label to the Detail section of a report, Access might display a trace error button. In the Detail section, labels in most cases are associated with controls that display data, so Access considers the addition of an independent label an error because it detects that the label is not associated with another control. You can ignore the error Access detects or select an option to create an association and then specify the field.

5

You can turn off the error-checking options related to labels on the Object Designers page of the Access Options dialog box.

See Also For information about setting a default format for labels, see "Manage labels" in "Objective 4.2: Configure form controls."

To add a label

1. Open the report in Design view or Layout view.

2. On the **Design** tool tab, in the **Controls** group, click **Controls**, and then click the **Label** control.

3. Click in the report where you want the label to appear.

4. Enter the text for the label.

To turn off error checking for labels

1. Open the **Access Options** dialog box, and display the **Object Designers** page.

2. In the **Error checking in form and report design view** section, clear the **Check for unassociated label and control** and **Check for new unassociated labels** check boxes.

3. Click **OK**.

Objective 5.2 practice tasks

The practice file for these tasks is located in the **MOSAccess2016\Objective5** practice file folder. The folder also contains a result file that you can use to check your work.

➤ Open the **Access_5-2** database. If the Info Bar opens below the ribbon, click the *Enable Content* button.

➤ Open the MyReport report in Layout view and do the following:

❏ From the Tasks table, add the following fields to the report: TaskID, CampaignID, TaskName, Description, and Status.

❏ Open the property sheet. From the Data tab, open the Query Builder for the Record Source property. Add the Comments table to the query design grid, and then add the Comment field to the first blank column in the design grid. Close the Query Builder, and confirm that you want to change the record source.

❏ Open the field list, and then add the Comment field to the report.

❏ Save and close the report.

➤ Open the Expense Summary report in Layout view and do the following:

❏ Group the report data by expense type and country/region.

❏ Sort the report by date purchased.

❏ Use the *Totals* button to sum the Amount Spent field. Select the option to show the group subtotal as a percentage of the grand total.

❏ Display the report in print preview, and then save and close the report.

➤ Open the Tasks report in Design view and do the following:

❏ Using the Controls group and the Subform/Subreport Wizard, add the CommentsSubreport as a subreport control below the existing fields.

❏ Change the *CommentsSubreport* label to *Comments*.

❏ Open the report in Report view to see your work, and then save and close the report.

➤ Open the **Access_5-2_results** database. Compare the two databases to check your work. Then close the open databases.

Objective 5.3: Format reports

You can use a variety of tools and techniques to format a report and the controls that you include on a report. For example, you can add an image, apply a theme to a report, or arrange a report's data in two or more columns. You can easily update the margins of the report and the spacing between controls. You can also use a calculated field in a report. This topic describes these and other aspects of formatting a report.

See Also For information about applying a theme to a report, positioning controls on a report, and inserting images, see "Objective 4.3: Format forms."

Apply page setup options

When a report is open in Design view or Layout view, you can format the report by changing its orientation (from landscape to portrait, for example), arranging the report's data in columns, and setting the page size and margins. You can specify these formatting options by using the options on the ribbon or by using the options in the Page Setup dialog box. For example, you can use the options in the Page Setup dialog box to apply custom margin settings instead of the standard settings Access provides.

When you want to set up a report in more than one column, you need to consider the number of fields the report contains, the width of report controls, and the page size. Columnar reports are best used for lists, directories, or other types of reports that include only a few fields. Stacking the fields (by using the stacked layout, for example) can also save space.

A three-column report

On the Columns tab of the Page Setup dialog box, you use the Grid Settings area to specify the number of columns and the space between rows and columns. The Width and Height boxes in the Column Size area adjust column dimensions. The Same As Detail option fits the columns within the Detail section of the report. You also specify a setting for the column layout so that the data in the columns runs down the page and then across or across the page and then down.

The options for a report's page size include Letter (8.5" × 11"), A4 (8.27" × 11.69"), and Legal (8.5" × 14"). Default settings for the margins for a report are Normal, Wide, and Narrow. You can refer to the dimensions Access displays and the simple preview to gauge how the margins affect the space provided for the report's data.

The Page Setup dialog box also includes the Print Options and Page tabs. You can set specific dimensions for a report's margins on the Print Options tab (instead of using the Normal, Wide, or Narrow options provided in the Page Size group). The Page tab provides options also available in the Page Layout and Page Size groups, including the Portrait and Landscape options for the report's page orientation and page size settings. If you want Access to use printer settings for a printer other than the default printer specified for your computer, specify that printer.

5

To specify column settings for a report

1. Open the report in Design view or Layout view.

2. On the **Page Setup** tool tab, in the **Page Layout** group, click **Columns**.

3. On the **Columns** tab of the **Page Setup** dialog box, specify the number of columns, the row and column spacing, the column size, and the column layout option, and then click **OK**.

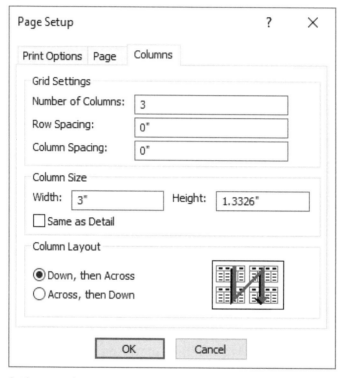

Setting up a columnar report

4. Display the report in print preview to test the settings.

To specify page size settings for a report

1. Open the report in Design view or Layout view.

2. On the **Page Setup** tool tab, in the **Page Size** group, do the following:

   a. Click **Size**, and then click an option for the report's page size.

   b. Click **Margins**, and then click one of the default options for page margins.

To specify page orientation for a report

1. Open the report in Design view or Layout view.

2. On the **Page Setup** tool tab, in the **Page Layout** group, click **Portrait** or **Landscape**.

Add a calculated field

In reports, you can use a calculated field to augment the information provided by the data fields. You can combine text fields by using the concatenation operator (the ampersand, &). For example, by using a calculated field of this type, you can display a contact's last name and first name in a single control, such as in the following example:

=*[First Name] & " " & [Last Name]*

You could also use the concatenation operator to create a custom label by using an expression such as the following:

=*"Please send your comments to " & [First Name]*

You can use the Expression Builder to help you create an expression by adding functions, operators, constants, and identifiers (which refer to the names of fields or tables, for example).

See Also For more information about the Expression Builder, see "Objective 3.3: Create calculated fields and grouping within queries."

By using arithmetic operators, you can add, subtract, multiply, or divide the values in numeric fields. For example, in a report that summarizes the amount spent in a specific budget category, you could divide that amount by the budget field to display the percentage spent of the total budget.

=*Sum([AmountSpent])/[CampaignBudget]*

Tip As shown in the examples in this section, enclose identifiers such as field names in square brackets.

To create a calculated field

1. Open the report in Design view or Layout view.

2. Add a text box control to the report, and then select that control.

3. Open the report property sheet. On the **Data** tab of the property sheet, click in the **Control Source** box, and then do one of the following.

   - Enter the expression that defines the calculated field.

   - Press **Shift+F2** to open the Zoom dialog box, and enter the expression in the dialog box.

   - Click the ellipsis in the **Control Source** box to open the Expression Builder for help writing the expression.

Format report elements

You can make changes to font properties for labels and other controls on a report. You can also change the size of the font, choose a different font color, or apply a background color to a control. Use the alignment buttons to position the text flush left, flush right, or centered.

Tip To select a report control for formatting, select the control from the Object list in the Selection group on the Format tool tab.

On the Format tool tab, in the Number group, you can apply a format to fields that use the Number, Currency, or Date/Time data type. The format you choose here affects how the date is displayed, but it does not change the date format specified for the field in the table.

With the commands in the Control Formatting group on the Format tool tab, you can format controls in other ways. The Shape Fill command adds a background color to a control such as the report's title. The Shape Outline command provides options for modifying the color and style of a control's borders.

Each control on a report, each report section, and the report itself has a group of properties that you can work with on the property sheet to format that report element. For a text box, you can set properties such as Width, Height, Back Color, Border Style, Border Color, Font Name, Font Size, and Text Align.

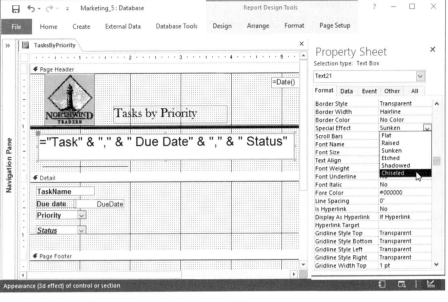

Setting the Special Effect property for a text box control

For report sections (such as Detail, Page Header, and Page Footer), you can set the Height property to 0 inches to hide the section. For the Detail section, you can set the Can Grow and Can Shrink properties to Yes if you want the size of the Detail section to increase and decrease depending on the amount of information it displays for a specific record. The Report Header and Report Footer sections also have these properties.

For the Report Header and Report Footer sections and the Page Header and Page Footer sections, you can also set the Display When property to Always, Print Only, or Screen Only. If you add page numbers to the Page Footer section, for example, set the Display When property to Print Only to show the page numbers only when you print the report.

Report properties include the Default View property, which controls whether the report opens in print preview or Report view by default. (The report opens in the view you specify for the Default View property when you right-click a report in the Navigation Pane and then click Open.)

5

To select controls on a report

→ On the report, select the control you want to format.

→ On the **Format** tool tab, in the **Selection** group, do either of the following:

- To select a specific control, expand the **Object** list, and then click the control you want to format.

- To select all controls on the report, click **Select All**.

To format report controls

1. Open the report in Design view or Layout view and select the control or controls you want to format.

2. On the **Format** tool tab, in the **Font** group, choose a new font, font size, or font color; apply bold, italic, or underline formatting; add a background fill color; and align the text.

3. For number, currency, and date and time fields, use the commands in the **Number** group on the **Format** tool tab to apply number, date/time, and currency formatting to the field.

4. In the **Control Formatting** group on the **Format** tool tab, do the following:

- Use the **Shape Fill** command to add a background fill color to a control.

- Use the **Shape Outline** command to apply line styles and colors to the control's borders.

To set control and report properties

1. Open the report in Design view or Layout view, and open the property sheet.

2. Select the control or report section you want to format.

3. In the property sheet, click in the box for the property you want to set, and then select an option Access provides or enter the value you want to use.

Add information to report headers and footers

In Design view and Layout view, you can use commands in the Header/Footer group of the Design tool tab to insert standard elements in a report's header and footer sections, including a logo, a title, the date and time, and page numbers.

The Page Numbers command opens a dialog box in which you select a format, position, and alignment for page numbers. Page numbers appear in the Page Header or Page Footer section and can be centered or aligned at the left or right border. You can clear the check box for the Show Number On First Page option to start pagination on the report's second page.

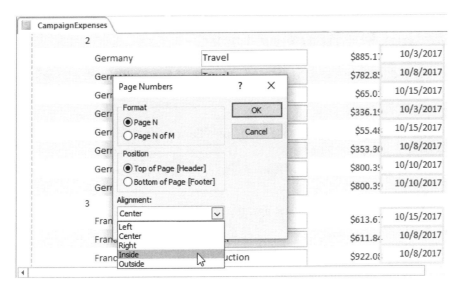

Alignment options for page numbers in a report

To insert information in a report header or footer

1. Open the report in Design view or Layout view.

2. On the **Design** tool tab, in the **Header/Footer** group, do any of the following:

   - To add a logo to the report header, click **Logo**. In the **Insert Picture** dialog box, navigate to and select the logo image file, and then click **Open**.

   - To add a title to the report header, click **Title**. In the **Auto_Header()** control that appears, replace the default title with the report title you want.

   - To add the date or time to the report header, click **Date and Time**. In the **Date and Time** dialog box, select the check boxes for the elements you want to include, select the element formats you want, and then click **OK**.

   - To add page numbers to the report header or footer, click **Page Numbers**. In the **Page Numbers** dialog box, click the format, position, and alignment you want. Then click **OK**.

5

Objective 5.3 practice tasks

The practice file for these tasks is located in the **MOSAccess2016\Objective5** practice file folder. The folder also contains a result file that you can use to check your work.

➤ Open the **Access_5-3** database. If the Info Bar opens below the ribbon, click the *Enable Content* button.

➤ Open the Expense Summary report in Layout view and do the following:

❑ Change the report page orientation to Landscape.

❑ Apply the *Integral* theme to only this report.

❑ Save and close the Expense Summary report.

➤ Open the Tasks report in Design view and do the following:

❑ Add the date and time to the report's header. Use the formats *DD-MMM-YY* and *HH:MM AM/PM*.

❑ Add a text box control below the TimeSpent field, and then create a calculated field that calculates the difference between the start date and the due date.

❑ Use the concatenation operator (&) to add the word <u>days</u> after the calculation.

❑ Change the field label to *Task Duration*.

❑ Save and close the report.

➤ Open the TasksByPriority report in Layout view and do the following:

❑ Set up a three-column report and set the column width to <u>6 inches</u>.

❑ Arrange the fields to go down, and then across.

❑ Apply bold formatting to the *TaskName*, *DueDate*, and *Priority* controls.

❑ Select the *Status* control, apply bold, italic, and underline formatting, and set the font color to Red.

❏ Select the calculated field in the page header, and set the Special Effect property to Shadowed.

❏ Display the report in print preview, and then save and close the report.

➤ Open the **Access_5-3_results** database. Compare the two databases to check your work, and then close the open databases.

Index

W

Web browser form control 153
Where function 131
worksheets, importing data from 10

X

XML files
    exporting data to 52–53
    importing 13
    importing data from 15
XPS files, saving queries as 117

Y

Yes/No field type 60

Z

zoom levels, previewing
  reports 47

About the author

 JOHN PIERCE is a freelance editor and writer. He is the author of *Team Collaboration: Using Microsoft Office for More Effective Teamwork* and other books about Microsoft Office, including the *MOS 2013 Study Guide for Microsoft Access*. John was an editor at Microsoft Press for 10 years and later worked as a technical writer at Microsoft, specializing in Microsoft SharePoint business solutions.

Now that you've read the book...

Tell us what you think!

Was it useful?
Did it teach you what you wanted to learn?
Was there room for improvement?

Let us know at https://aka.ms/tellpress

Your feedback goes directly to the staff at Microsoft Press,
and we read every one of your responses. Thanks in advance!

 Microsoft